Contents

1. MPS-001: UNIT-1: What is Political Theory & Why Study It ?

- Introduction
- What is Political Theory ? – It's Implications and Contents
- Nature of Political Theory – as History, as Philosophy, as Science
- Political Theory: Growth & Evaluation – Classical, Modern, Contemporary
- Why Study Political Theory? – Tasks Before Political Theory, Significance of Political Theory

IGNOU Book Exercise & Past 8 Attempts Questions - IMPORTANT

- ❑ **IGNOU BOOK EXERCISE**
- ❑ **PAST 8 ATTEMPTS IGNOU QUESTIONS**

Dec 2020: **"Modern political theory attempted to build a Science of Politics." In the light of this statement, discuss the features of Modern Political Theory.**

 Political theory has, in the West, passed through different stages. There was a time when, during the **ancient Greek** and the medieval period, political theory would concern itself with identifying the ethical goals of the state, i.e., the objectives which the state would cherish to achieve.

Both **Plato and Aristotle** would insist on the functions of the state to establish justice or give the individual, a good life.

The **medieval** political theory associated as it was with religion, demanded of the state to prepare and train the individual to seek a place with god.

The **early modern age** political theory sought to discuss theories of the origin of the state, followed by philosophers with whom the organisation and functions of the state were major concerns of the state.

The **mid 20th century** political theory dealt largely with the institutions of the state, making the concept of power to be the basic theme of the state.

The growth and evolution of political theory can be elaborated in three major streams. These are: (i) classical political theory, (ii) modern political theory, and (iii) contemporary political theory.

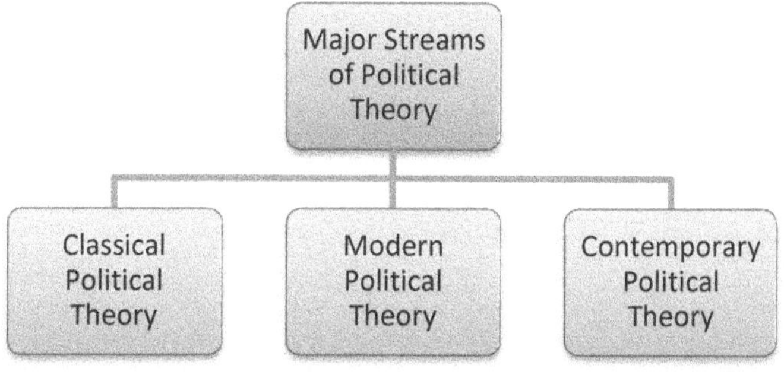

Modern political theory encompasses in itself a host of diverse trends such as the institutional-structural, scientific, positivistic, empirical, behavioural, post-behavioural and the Marxist.

Modern political theory, beginning with the liberal stance from the 15th-16th centuries and later expressing itself in the institutional-positivist, empirical-behavioural and post-behavioural trends, dubbed the **whole classical tradition as dull**.

Modern political theory with its western liberal-democratic shade attempted to build a science of politics; objective, empirical, observational, measurable, operational and value-free. Its features can be summed up as under:

(i) Facts and data constitute the bases of study. These are accumulated, explained and then used for testing hypothesis.

(ii) Human behaviour can be studied, and regularities of human behaviour can be expressed in generalisations.

(iii) Subjectivity gives way to objectivity; philosophical interpretation to analytical explanation; purpose to procedure; descriptive to observational; normative to scientific.

(iv) Facts and values are separated; values are so arranged that the facts become relevant.

(v) Methodology has to be self-conscious, explicit and quantitative.

(vi) Inter-disciplinary synthesis is to be achieved.

(vii)"What it is" is regarded as more important than either "what it was" or "what it ought to be or could be".

(viii) Values are to support facts, substance to form, and theory to research, and status quo to social change.

At the other end of modern political theory stands the Marxist political theory, also called the 'dialectical-materialist' or the 'scientific-socialist' theory. It describes the general laws of motion in the development of all phenomena.

<u>Dec 2018 & Dec 2019:</u> Discuss the meaning and nature of political Theory. Discuss the significance of political theory.

Answer by India Ebook: Political Theory is not only a theory of/about politics, it also the science of politics, the philosophy of politics as at. Political Theory is **not** fantasy, though it may contain an element of political vision.

It is **not** politicking, though it does take account political realities for its study and analysis.

It is **not** all scientism, though it seeks to reach the roots of all political activity analytically and systematically.

It is **not** ideology, though it attempts to justify a political system & condemns another.

It is theoretical, scientific, philosophical & at the same time dynamic with a clear objective of attaining a better social order.

It thus, has in varying degrees, elements of THEORY, SCIENCE, PHILOSOPHY and IDEOLOGY

To know clearly as what Political Theory really is, is to know its nature. Political theory is *said to be political thought*, and that is why there are some who describe political theory as denoting the works of numerous thinkers. **But it is not what political thought is.**

There are others who equate political theory with political philosophy. It is true that political theory constitutes a part of political philosophy, but it is only a part.

Political theory is not all history, but in the limited sense; it is **not all philosophy**, but it is philosophy in some degree; it is **not all science**, but it is science in so far as it responds to reason. A political theorist has to be a part historian, a part philosopher, and a part scientist.

❑ POLITICAL THEORY AS HISTORY

Political Science is very closely related to History. Hence, Political Science always takes the help of History for studying political institutions i.e. the history of their evolution from their emergence and gradual evolution into their contemporary forms, powers, functions, mutual relations and relative positions.

History is **more than the tale** of the *dead* and the *buried*; it is **store-house** of **experience and wisdom**; **successes and failures**, of **what** has been **achieved**, and **what** has been **lost.**

Political theory as a History defines what **has lost its value**. No one cries now that the state has been a divine creation or the result of a contract in the state of nature.

As history, political theory conserves what has significance and helps posterity to cherish it for a long time to come.

Political theory is History in the sense that it seeks to understand the time, the place and the circumstances in which it evolves.

If it ignores its historical context, it loses its strength, focus & message.

Political theory **without history is a structure without a base**. In studying and analysing politics, what we learn to understand is a political tradition, and a concrete way of behaviour. It is, therefore, proper that the study of politics should essentially be a historical study.

Political theory is not merely or only history, it is a **Science in so far as it is not understood in isolation**, and **also a philosophy in so far as it motivates.**

❏ POLITICAL THEORY AS PHILOSOPHY

The main purpose of political philosophy is to establish a **general value** about the state and **political life**. Political philosophy follows a normative approach to the analysis of the state and political life.

Philosophy, as an abstract study encompassing the **whole universe in general, and morals, norms, and values in particular, is the sum-total of general laws governing the whole world.**

Political theory is a Philosophy, for it not only seeks to know the nature of things but also attempts to explain as to why things really exist. One understands an action or a thought only by evaluating it. Evaluation is a part of understanding.

Political theory as philosophy is "the attempt truly to know both the nature of political things and the right, or the good, political order." (by - Leo Strauss)

Politics is not what one Assumes or Opines. In fact, a political theorist is expected to possess more than an assumption or an opinion; he has to have knowledge. Philosophy emerges when opinion/assumption attains the heights of knowledge, and that is what exactly is the task of political theory.

Political theory as Philosophy is an, "attempt to replace opinion/assumption about the nature of political things by knowledge of the nature of political things.

❑ POLITICAL THEORY AS SCIENCE

Political theory is a science has been forcefully emphasized by Scholars from Arthur Bentley to George Catlin; David Easton and Robert Dahl; but all science is not political theory, just as all political theory is not science.

Political Theory is not science in the sense Chemistry or Physics or Mathematics is a science. It is not as exact a science as these natural or physical sciences are, because there are no universally recognised principles, no clear cause-effect relationships, no laboratories and no predictions are made in political theory the way these are found in natural and exact sciences.

Political Theory as a science is only a social science. It is science in its methodology, in its approach & in its analysis. The role of science in political theory should be limited to the extent that it helps understand a political phenomenon.

The **significance of political theory** has been under a cloud by scholars, mostly of the behaviouralist school. According to **John Plamenatz**, political theory has its uses which may be stated as under:

(i) Political theory is a serious and difficult intellectual activity and the need for this kind of exercise, in modern times, is indeed much greater.

(ii) It is a study of values, norms and goals, though it does not produce the same kind of knowledge as empirical political theory does.

(iii) It is a study of theories which have, historically, powerfully influenced men's images of themselves, and of society, and profoundly determined their social and political behaviour.

(iv) It has an element of socially conditioned ideology. This ideology may be an illusion, and yet, unless man had these illusions, the course of social development would not have been what it is.

(v) It produces a coherent system of political principles which can guide us to an appropriate political action.

2. MPS-001: UNIT-2: Democracy

- Introduction: The Origins of the Democratic Ideal
- Historical Background
- The Conceptual Family of Democracy: Autonomy, Equality and Liberty
- Justifications for Democracy: Intrinsic and Instrumental
- Democracy: Procedural and Substantive
- Types of Democracy: Representative, Participatory, Deliberative, Social and Cosmopolitan Democracy

IGNOU Book Exercise & Past 8 Attempts Questions - IMPORTANT

❑ **IGNOU BOOK EXERCISE**

Q. 2 Explain the evolution and growth of democracy in the 20th Century.

Answer by India Ebook: A democracy is a **political system**, or a **system of decision-making** within an institution or organization or a country, in which **all members have an equal share of power.**

Democracy is generally **associated** with the **efforts of the ancient Greeks**, who 18th century intellectuals considered the founders of Western civilization.

The concepts (and name) of democracy and constitution as a form of government **originated** in **ancient Athens circa 508 B.C. (2500 years ago)**

In ancient Greece, where there were **many city-states** with <u>different forms of government</u>, democracy was contrasted with governance by **elites** (aristocracy), **by one person** (monarchy), **by tyrants** (tyranny), etc.

Democracy has been described as one of the **"characteristic institutions of modernity",** and as such it was the result of a complex and intertwined processes of ideological, social and economic change.

The main **difference** between **Ancient & Modern Democracy**, is in the way in which *'the people'* were defined. In Ancient Greek Polity, the 'Demos' was rather restrictively defined, and notably **excluded three(3)** main **categories of persons**: *Slaves, Women & Metics* (the foreigners who lived & worked in the city-state)

The actual career of Athenian democracy was fairly troubled, as aristocrats, generals & demagogues made periodic attempts to control power. Their contempt for the poor – described as 'the mob' or 'the rabble' – finds echoes in the modern World, were democracy achieved through struggle, & against considerable odds.

Indeed, the **struggle for democracy everywhere & throughout history**, has been simultaneously a struggle against political inequality based on, & justified by, inequalities of birth and Wealth.

The **20th century** saw an unparalleled extension of democracy in terms of both its *inclusiveness* as well as its *spatial expansion*. Beginning with the extension of the suffrage to women in the older western democracies, and ending with the dismantling of apartheid in South Africa, democracy in the 20th century became more inclusive.

This phenomenon has been described in terms of **"waves of democratisation"**. The democratisation of many countries in Europe in the 19TH century is viewed as the **first wave** of democratisation.

The **second wave** is dated to the period following **World War I**, when many countries of Europe – including those of **Scandinavia** - became democratic.

The **third wave** of democracy came after the **Second World War**, when new democracies were established in countries like **Germany and Italy** after the collapse of Nazism and Fascism; and following **de-colonisation** in the **1950s and 1960s**, democracy was eagerly **adopted** by most of the new nations of **Asia and Africa.**

The **fourth wave** of democratisation saw a return to democracy in **post-Communist Eastern Europe**, as well as in many countries of **Latin America** that had turned their backs on democracy.

Q.4 Explain various types of Democracy.

Answer by India Ebook: The following are the various types of Democracy:

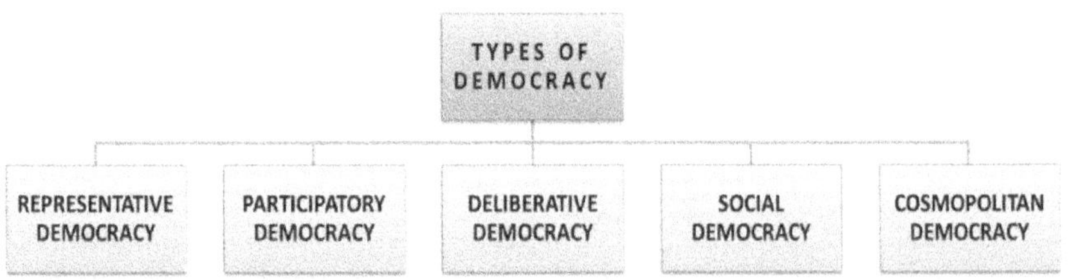

REPRESENTATIVE DEMOCRACY & ITS CRITICS

Since **direct democracy is not possible** in large and complex societies, the mechanism through which people take part **indirectly in government** is through **electing representatives** to carry out their will.

Representative democracy can function as **an element of both** the **parliamentary** and the **presidential systems of government**. It typically manifests in a **lower chamber** such as the **House of Commons of the United Kingdom**, and **the Lok Sabha of India**, but may be curtailed by constitutional constraints such as an upper chamber and judicial review of legislation.

Be that as it may, today representative government - based on the majority principle - is considered the best way of giving effect to the democratic impulse. It has, however, **two types of critics**, those who consider **it unrealistic** (Schumpeter and the elite theorists) and those who consider **it inadequate** (participatory democrats, discussed in the next section).

The headers used in Body text are 'Book title' on the left-side page and 'Author name' or 'Chapter name' on the right-side page. Pages in which chapters start would not have headers or footers.

PARTICIPATORY DEMOCRACY

Participatory democracy or participative democracy is a model of democracy in which **citizens are provided power to make political**

decisions. It tends to **advocate greater citizen participation** and **more direct representation** than traditional representative democracy.

E.g, the **creation of governing bodies** through a system of **sortition** (also known as selection by lottery/lot/allotment), rather than election of representatives, is thought to produce a more participatory body by allowing citizens to hold positions of power themselves.

DELIBERATIVE DEMOCRACY

It values open & public deliberation on issues of common concern. It starts from the assumption of individuals as Autonomous persons, but does not view the social relationships between these autonomous persons as relationships of conflict or interest.

SOCIAL DEMOCRACY

Social democracy is a political, social, and economic philosophy within socialism that supports political and economic democracy.

It is a form of democracy that is based on a strong commitment to equality. Social democrats, therefore, support the idea of the welfare state based on redistribution.

They believe in the liberal institutions of representative democracy, but wish to combine these with the ideal of social justice.

COSMOPOLITAN DEMOCRACY

Cosmopolitan democracy is a political theory which explores the application of norms and values of democracy at the **transnational and global sphere**. It argues that global governance of the people, by the people, for the people is possible and needed.

❏ PAST 8 ATTEMPTS IGNOU QUESTIONS
June 2022; Assess Democracy as a form of government.

Answer by India Ebook: The word "Democracy" came from the **Greek** word "Demokratia" – is a combination of the words 'Demos' (meaning the people) and 'Kratos' (meaning rule).

This **gives democracy** its meaning **as a form of Government** in **which the people rule**, whether **directly** – through personal participation – **or indirectly**, through elected representatives.

To understand "Democracy" in-depth, we have to understand "Republic". **India is a Democratic Republic.**

The main **difference** between **Ancient & Modern Democracy**, is in the way in which *'the people'* were defined. In Ancient Greek Polity, the 'Demos' was rather restrictively defined, and notably **excluded three(3)** main **categories of persons**: *Slaves, Women & Metics* (the foreigners who lived & worked in the city-state)

The actual career of Athenian democracy was fairly troubled, as aristocrats, generals & demagogues made periodic attempts to control power. Their contempt for the poor – described as 'the mob' or 'the rabble' – finds echoes in the modern World, were democracy achieved through struggle, & against considerable odds.

Indeed, the **struggle for democracy everywhere & throughout history**, has been simultaneously a struggle against political inequality based on, & justified by, inequalities of birth and Wealth.

In large and complex societies, it is **not always possible** for people to gather together to make decisions on each & every issue, as they did in the direct democracy of ancient Athens. This is why modern democracy works through representative institutions. **People elect their representatives to a legislature or assembly,** and these representatives are authorised to take decisions on behalf of those who elected them.

However, democracy should **not** be seen merely as a **set of institutions** - e.g., free and fair elections, legislative assemblies, & constitutional governments arising out of these. This view of democracy is described as

procedural democracy, because it emphasizes only the procedures and institutions of democracy.

Social & economic inequalities make it difficult for a formal participation to be effective. This is why **theorists emphasize** the importance of **substantive democracy.** This ideal suggests a society of truly equal citizens, who are politically engaged, tolerant of different opinions and ways of life, & have an equal voice in choosing their rulers & holding them accountable.

June 2021: "Democracy is beautiful in theory: in practice it is a fallacy." Discuss the merits and demerits of Democracy in the light of this statement.

Answer by India Ebook: A democracy is a **political system**, or a **system of decision-making** within an institution or organization or a country, in which **all members have an equal share of power.**

Democracy is generally **associated** with the **efforts of the ancient Greeks**, who 18th century intellectuals considered the founders of Western civilization.

The concepts (and name) of democracy and constitution as a form of government **originated** in **ancient Athens circa 508 B.C. (2500 years ago)**

In ancient Greece, where there were **many city-states** with different forms of government, democracy was contrasted with governance by **elites** (aristocracy), **by one person** (monarchy), **by tyrants** (tyranny), etc.

Democracy is a political structure in which people directly exercise power, or elect members from among themselves to represent the people, such as a parliament. It is also called the majority rule and here can't inherit the power. People are choosing their representatives. Representatives participate in an election and the voters elect their member. Democracy is a form of government in which:

- Rulers elected by the people take all the major decisions

- Elections offer a choice and fair opportunity to the people to change the current rulers

- This choice and opportunity is available to all the people on an equal basis

- The exercise of this choice leads to a government limited by basic rules of the constitution and citizens' rights

Merits of democracy

i) A democratic government is a more responsible form of government, is a stronger form of government.

ii) The standard of making decisions is improved by democracy.

iii) The integrity of people is strengthened by democracy.

iv) The wealthy and educated have the same standing as the poor and less educated.

v) Democracy helps us to fix our own mistakes.

Demerits of democracy

a) Leaders keep changing in a democracy leading to instability
b) Democracy is all about political competition and power play, leaving no scope for morality
c) Many people have to be consulted in a democracy that leads to delays
d) Elected leaders do not know the best interest of the people, resulting in bad decisions
e) Democracy leads to corruption since it is based on electoral competition
f) Ordinary people don't know what is good for them; they should not decide anything

Dec 2019: Distinguish between Procedural and Substantive democracy.

Answer by India Ebook: Refer **MPS-003**: India: Democracy & Development **UNIT-27**.

3. MPS-001: UNIT-3: Rights

- ➤ Introduction
- ➤ Rights: Meaning & Nature – Rights, Claims & Powers, Meaning of Rights, Nature of Rights
- ➤ Theories of Rights – Theory of Natural Rights, Legal Rights, The Historical Theory of Rights, The Social Welfare Theory of Rights, The Marxist Theory of Rights
- ➤ Framework of Rights – Rights of the People, Laski's Theory of Rights, Theory of Human Rights

IGNOU Book Exercise & Past 8 Attempts Questions - IMPORTANT

❏ IGNOU BOOK EXERCISE

Q.1 What do you mean by rights? Distinguish between rights, power, claims and entitlements.

Answer by India Ebook: Rights are rightly called **social claims** which help individuals attain their best selves and help them develop their personalities.

If democracy is to be government of the people, it has to exist for them. Such a democratic government can best serve the people if it maintains a system of rights for its people.

States never give rights, they only recognise them; governments never grant rights, they only protect them. Rights emanate from society, from peculiar social conditions, and, therefore, they are always social.

Rights are **legal, social,** or **ethical principles** of <u>freedom or entitlement</u>; that is, rights are the *fundamental normative rules* about what is allowed of people or owed to people according to some legal system, social convention, or ethical theory.

Rights **belong to the individuals,** and therefore, **they are not of the state.** Rights are individuals' rights, and, therefore, they are conditions necessary for their development. Rights are the products of our social nature, and as such, the result of our membership of the society.

RIGHTS, CLAIMS AND POWERS

Rights are indeed claims, **but every claim is not a right. A claim is not a right if it is not recognised; it is not a right if it is not enforced.** Claims which are not recognised are empty claims; claims *not enforced* are *powerless claims*.

Claims become rights when they **are recognised by society**; they become rights when they are maintained and enforced by the state.

Rights are not merely claims, they are social claims. They are not claims, but they are in the nature of claims. What this means is that claims which are social in nature, alone are rights.

Rights as social claims presuppose the existence of the society. **There are no rights (i.e. social claims) where there is no society.**

Rights as social claims have to have another requisite. They are to be maintained, enforced and protected. It is here that the institution of the state has a definite role to play. It is society and not the state, that rewards individuals after their having performed their duties, with their rights.

Rights are social claims; they are not powers. Rights and powers have to be distinguished. Nature has bestowed every individual with a certain amount of power to satisfy his/her needs.

Power is a physical force; it is sheer energy. On the basis of mere force, no system of rights can be established. If a person has power, it does not necessarily mean that he has a right.

Q.2 Briefly describe the various theories of rights.

Answer by India Ebook: **There are numerous theories of rights** which explain the nature, origin and meaning of rights. The theory of natural rights describes rights as nature; the theory of legal rights recognises rights as legal; the historical theory of rights pronounces rights as products of traditions and customs; the idealistic theory, like the theory of legal rights, relates rights only with the state; the social welfare theory of rights regards rights as social to be exercised in the interest of both the individual and the society.

THEORY OF NATURAL OF RIGHTS

The theory of natural rights has been advocated mainly by **Thomas Hobbes** (Leviathan, 1651), **John Locke** (Two Treatises on Government, 1690) and **J.J. Rousseau** (The Social Contract, 1762).

These contractualists, after having provided the social contract theory, hold the view that there were **natural rights possessed** by men in the state of nature and that these rights were attributed to individuals as if they were the essential properties of men as men. The contractualists, therefore, declared that the rights are inalienable, imprescriptable and indefeasible.

The theory of **natural rights is criticised** on many **grounds.** Rights cannot be natural simply because they were the possessions of men in the state of nature.

For **Bentham**, the doctrine of natural rights was 'a rhetorical non-sense upon stilts.' **Laski also rejects** the whole idea of natural rights. Rights, as natural rights, are based on false assumptions that we can have rights and duties independently of society.

Burke had pointed out, rather eloquently, when he said that we cannot enjoy the rights of civil and uncivil state at the same time: the more perfect the natural rights are in the abstract, the more difficult it is to recognise them in practice.

THEORY OF LEGAL OF RIGHTS

The idealist theory of rights which seeks to place rights as the product of the state can be, more or less, seen as another name of the theory of legal rights. Among the advocates of such theories, the names of **Bentham, Hegel and Austin** can be mentioned.

According to them, rights are granted by the state, regarding rights as a claim which the force of the state grants to the people. The **essential features** of these **theories**, then, are:

(i) the state defines and lays down the bill of rights: rights are neither prior nor anterior to the state because it is the state which is the source of rights;

(ii) the state lays down a legal framework which guarantees rights and that it is the state which enforces the enjoyment of rights;

(iii) as the law creates and sustains rights, so when the content of law changes, the substance of rights also changes.

THE HISTORICAL THEORY OF RIGHTS

The historical theory of rights, also called the **prescriptive** theory, regards the state as the product of a long historical process. It holds the view that rights grow from traditions & customs.

As **traditions and customs** stabilise owing to their constant and continuous usage, they take the shape of rights. The theory has its origins in the **18th century** in the writings of **Edmund Burke** and was adopted later by the sociologists.

The historical theory of rights is important in so far as **it condemns the legal theory of rights**. It is also important in so far as it denies the theory of natural rights. The state recognises, the advocates of the historical theory of rights argue, what (the rights including) comes to stay through long usage.

The historical theory of rights suffers from its **own limitations**. It cannot be admitted that all our customs result in rights: the **Sati system** does **not constitute** a right nor does infanticide. All our rights do not have their origins in customs. Right to social security, for example, is not related to any custom.

THE SOCIAL WELFARE THEORY OF RIGHTS

The **theory argues** that the state should recognise only such rights as **help promote social welfare.** Among the modern advocates of the social welfare theory, the name of **Roscoe Pound** and **Chafee** can be mentioned though Bentham can be said to be its advocate of the **18th century.**

The theory implies that rights are the **creation of the society** in as much as they are based on the consideration of common welfare: rights are the conditions of social good which means that claims not in conformity with the general welfare, and therefore, not recognised by the community do not become our rights.

The social welfare theory of rights is also **not without its faults**. It dwells on the factor of social welfare, a term too vague to be precise. The Benthamite formula 'greatest good of the greatest number' is different to different people. The theory turns out to be the legal theory of rights if, in the end, the state is to decide what constitutes 'social welfare'.

THE MARXIST THEORY OF RIGHTS

The Marxist theory of rights is understood in terms of the economic system at a particular period of history. A particular socio-economic formation would have a particular system of rights. The state, being an instrument in the hands of the economically dominant class, is itself a class institution and the law which it formulates is also a class law. So considered, the feudal state, through feudal laws, protects the system of rights (privileges, for example) favouring the feudal system.
According to Marx, the class which controls the economic structure of society also controls political power and it uses this power to protect and promote its own interests rather than the interests of all.

Q.4 Discuss Harold Laski's Theory of Rights.

Answer by India Ebook: **Laski's Theory of Rights**
Harold Laski (1893-1950), a theoretician of the **English Labour Party** and a Political Scientist in his own right, has his definite views on the system of rights as expounded in his **A Grammar of Politics** (first published in 1925 and then revised almost every second year).

❑ **Laski's views** on the **nature of rights** run as follows:

(i) they are social conditions, given to the individual as a member of the society

(ii) they help promote individual personality, his best-self: 'those social conditions without which no man can seek to be his best self'

(iii) they are social because they are never against social welfare; they were not there before the emergence of society

(iv) the state only recognises and protects rights by maintaining them;

(v) rights are never absolute: absolute rights are a contradiction in terms

(vi) they are dynamic in nature in so far as their contents change according to place, time and conditions

(vii) they go along with duties; in fact, duties are prior to rights; the exercise of rights implies the exercise of duties.

❑ PAST 8 ATTEMPTS IGNOU QUESTIONS

June 2021: Write short note on: (a) Theory of Natural Rights

Answer by India Ebook: Almost same as **Q.2** of the Above.

Dec 2020: Write short note on: (a) Legal Theory of Right

Answer by India Ebook: Almost same as **Q.2** of the Above.

June 2020: Examine the theory of Natural Rights

Answer by India Ebook: Almost same as **Q.2** of the Above.

June 2019: Describe briefly various theories of rights.

Answer by India Ebook: Exact same as Q.2 of the Above (as it was asked for 20 marks name all 5 theories of rights and expain them very briefly)

4. MPS-001: UNIT-4: Liberty

- Introduction
- Negative Liberty
- Positive Liberty
- Recent Debates on Liberty

IGNOU Book Exercise & Past 8 Attempts Questions - IMPORTANT

- **IGNOU BOOK EXERCISE**
- **PAST 8 ATTEMPTS IGNOU QUESTIONS**

Dec 2019: Examine some of the recent debates on Liberty.

Answer by India Ebook: Now that we have covered the **traditional debate** over freedom between the negative and positive liberty advocates, let us look at some ideological positions which are tangential to this debate. We will now look at how feminism has grappled with the value of freedom.

It has been claimed that "Freedom began its long journey in the Western consciousness as a woman's value". Women constituted the first slaves in the period of rudimentary state formation in **late ninth and eight century B.C. Greece**.

During the **constant warfare** between the aristocratic clans of that period, *male prisoners of war were killed*, while women were enslaved. As the **first slaves in early Greek society**, women, both those who were actually slaves, and those who lived in dread of capture and enslavement, thought of, and valued the condition antithetical to that of slavery - that of freedom.

As slaves, ancient Greek women imagined being able to assert their own will once they were free, but as women-slaves, they visualised the state of freedom not as the domination of the will of others, but as a state to be shared with others. For them, freedom was love, a condition of being restored to their kin's folk and families.

This **concern** with an **alternative women's conception of freedom** has become **dominant** in the writings of the post 1960s women's movement in the west.

The **mother** who is the **primary caretaker**, represents the entire world outside the self, that is, the object world, to all infants, and the relationship with his or her mother determines a child's response to others in the world: the infant's stance toward itself and the world-all derive in the first instance from this earliest relationship. In their first few years of life human infants go through different phases - symbiosis, separation and individuation - in their relationship with their mother. Male and female infants in a patriarchal culture, experience these phases differently because their mothers, for psychological and sociological reasons, respond to them differently.

Mothers are able, for instance, to more easily encourage the separation and individuation of their sons, while being less willing to give up the symbiotic phase with respect to their daughters.

In addition little boys soon learn to fear their primary identification with their mothers because they realise that their male identity is defined as not being like a female.

These psychological processes have an effect on their relationships with others in general: the attainment of masculine gender identity involves denial of attachment or relationship.

This process of psychological development in childhood has been used to explain adult male responses, for example, the apparent male perception of all relationships as threatening, and their sense of freedom as the absence of the (m) other.

By doing so, it also problematises the prevalent norms for selfhood and autonomy, which are supposed to be based on the experiences of men. It is misguided to conceptualise the realisation of autonomy or freedom as requiring the absence of others. The development of autonomy takes place in interaction with other selves, and therefore freedom needs to be conceptualised in terms other than non-interference.

Pateman is thus a critic of contract and claims that women's freedom can be constructed only by giving up the language of contract. This language encourages a conception of individuals as having property in their person, and its corollary is to see freedom as independence, specially the independence of participating in the labour market.

Pateman continues this argument in a later piece, arguing that 'freedom as independence' should be transformed into 'freedom as autonomy', a freedom that is secured through the recognition of the interdependence of all citizens.

The above discussion referred to the treatment of freedom in one specific ideological tradition. If we, however, look at another ideological position, for instance, the liberal-communitarian debate, we can see similar controversies about the meaning of individual liberty.

5. MPS-001: UNIT-5: Equality

- Introduction
- Equality vs. Inequality – Struggle for Equality
- What is Equality?
- **Dimensions Equality: Legal, Political , Economic, Social**
- Relation of Equality with Liberty and Justice
    - Equality & Liberty As Opposed to each other
    - Equality & Liberty are Complementary to each other
    - Equality and Justice
- Towards Equality
- Plea for Inequality in the Contemporary World
- Marxist Concept of Equality

IGNOU Book Exercise & Past 8 Attempts Questions - IMPORTANT

❑ **IGNOU BOOK EXERCISE**

2. Discuss different dimensions of equality.

Answer by India Ebook: Equality is a multi-dimensional concept. The need for equality is felt in different fields of social life.

Historically also, the demand for different dimensions of equality was neither raised simultaneously nor with the same intensity. While liberalism laid more emphasis on legal-political dimensions of equality, the socialists preferred socio-economic equality. The different dimensions of equality are:

❑ **Legal Equality**

❑ **Political Equality**

❑ **Economic Equality**

❑ **Social Equality**

Legal Equality is defined as equality before law, equal subjection of all to the same legal code and equal opportunity for all to secure legal protection of their rights and freedom. There should rule of law and laws must be equally binding for all. In every society equality must be ensured in all these forms.

a) Equality before Law consists in 'equal subject of all classes to the ordinary law of the land administered by the ordinary law courts'. It means that amongst equals, the law should be equal and should be equally administered and that the 'like should be treated alike'.

b) Equal Protection of Law: It means 'equal laws for equals and unequal laws for unequals'. This can be understood very well in the context of the Indian constitution where the law, while not recognising any distinction based upon birth, caste, creed or religion, does accept certain rational discriminations like reservation of seats or special queues for ladies, concessions given to students in railway journeys etc. Such discrimination based upon backwardness, sex, ability etc. are considered rational discriminations. In such cases, law protects the people by unequal rather than equal application.

Political Equality is referred **as equal opportunities** for participation of all in the political process. This involves the concept of **grant of equal political rights** for all the citizens with **some uniform** qualifications for everyone.

All **citizens must possess similar political rights**, they should have similar voice in the working of the government and they should have equal opportunities to actively participate in the political life and affairs of the country. Political equality guarantees the enjoyment of similar political rights to all citizens.

Universal **adult franchise is a means to this end.** Universal adult suffrage has been introduced in **India**. The same provision has been made in **England, U.S.S.R., U.S.A., France** and many other countries.

Economic equality does not indicate that equal treatment or equal reward or equal wages for **all.** It denotes to fair and adequate opportunities to *all for work and for earning* of their livelihoods. It also means that primary needs of all should be fulfilled before the special needs of few are gratified. The gap between rich and poor should be lowest. There should be equitable distribution of wealth and resources in the society.

Economic Equality is **closely associated to political equality**. Professor **Laski** stated the immense significance of economic equality. *"Political equality is never real unless, it is accompanied with virtual economic liberty; political power"*.

Generally, economic equality mean the provision of equal opportunities to all so they may be able to make their economic progress. This can be done **only** in **Socialism** and **not in Capitalism**. Henceforth, Capitalism should be replaced by Socialism.

Social equality is referred as equal rights and opportunities for development for all classes of people without any discrimination such as civil rights, freedom of speech, property rights, and equal access to social goods and services.

However**, it also includes** concepts of health equity, economic equality and other social securities. It also includes equal opportunities and obligations, and so involves the whole of society. Social equality requires the absence of legally enforced social class or caste boundaries and the absence of discrimination motivated by an inalienable part of a person's identity. For instance, sex, gender, race, age, sexual orientation, origin, caste or class, income or property, language, religion, convictions, opinions, health or disability must not result in unsatisfactory treatment under the law and should not reduce opportunities unreasonably.

3.   Explain the relation of equality with liberty and justice.

Answer by India Ebook: The relation between **equality and liberty** has been one of the interesting controversies of liberalism. The root of the controversy is: **Are liberty and equality opposed to each other or are they complimentary to each other?**

In the modern constitutions, we find a frequent association of both liberty and equality in the list of fundamental rights. But they have not always been the same.

❑ **Liberty and Equality As Opposed to Each Other**

That _liberty and equality_ are opposed to each other has been an important _current of early liberalism._ Classical liberalism gave so much importance to liberty that equality became a slave of it. It believed that liberty is natural and so is equality. So by nature liberty and equality are opposed to each other.

In other words, the **price of significant equality would be political despotism which would subordinate individual talent and achievement.** In the name of equality, the state unnecessarily increases its powers and restricts the rights and liberties of the people.

❑ **Liberty and Equality As Opposed to Each Other**

Radical equality of persons and outcome requires a totalitarian system of regulation. However, even this is no guarantee to equality.

In short, liberty and equality are incompatible, liberalism stands for liberty, equality is desirable only before law, political equality should be limited to the right to vote and elections of the elite; social and economic equality in so far as it increases the powers of the state is a threat to liberty.

❑ **Equality and Liberty Are Complimentary To Each Other**

The early liberal argument that equality and liberty are mutually exclusive assumed an inevitable conflict between personal interests and social requirements. But this dichotomy of individual versus society proved false historically. The demand for economic and social equality raised in the 19th century by the socialists and positive liberals made equality the prime requirement of liberty. Positive liberals maintained that liberty and equality are complementary to each other and the state was assigned the task of correcting the social and economic imbalances through legislation and regulation.

❑ **Equality and Liberty Are Complimentary To Each Other**

Positive liberalism saw the <u>individual as a social being</u> whose personal desires could be satisfied in the context of a cooperative social relationship within a social environment.

Without the satisfaction of economic needs, liberty cannot be realised. In a society of economic unequals, gross inequalities make liberty the privilege of a few.

Positive liberals did not agree with the view that state regulations in the economic and social spheres will lead to authoritarianism.

However, **inspite of reconciliation between liberty and equality**, even positive liberalism prefers liberty to equality. For example, Barker writes that whatever claims be made in the name of equality, it cannot be viewed in isolation, for the principle stands by the principles of liberty and fraternity.

But still there are **reasons for thinking** that liberty matters even more than equality. It is greater because it is more closely connected with the supreme value of the personality than the spontaneous development of its capacities.

4.   Discuss the role of equality in contemporary societies.

Answer by India Ebook: There is no doubt that all societies are unequal. The rise of capitalism replaced one set ofinequalities based upon birth and privileges with another set of inequalities based upon privateproperty; yet there are a number of historical changes which promoted trends towards equalityand egalitarianism.

We can say that in a world of inequalities, there are trends which promote equalityin human societies. Firstly, there is a sense of justice which appears to be a necessary featureof all social relations. Inequality is on the defensive. Secondly, the politics of democratic societiesis not coercive control, but a set of institutions which enable people to achieve desired goals.Thirdly, social groups and movements such as the working class and the feminist movementssuccessfully mobilise to achieve substantive social rights.

Equality is a relative concept and has to be understood in the context ofprevailing inequalities. Inequality is a universal feature of all societies and its opposition has beenfundamental to all social relations.

Yet, inequality is still legitimised in contemporary society byreference to a variety of ideological systems which explain the necessity and legitimacy of allforms of inequality. Hence, in order to understand equality, it is desirable to know the argumentsagainst equality.

Most forms of traditional ideology legitimising inequality between persons have been religiousin character. For example, all major religions – whether Hinduism, Buddhism, Confucianism –believed in the transmission of a special type of knowledge to a cultural elite via a period of training and adherence to rituals which guaranteed purity. Virtually all religions are grounded inthe notion of inequality.

If Hinduism justified varna-system, similar was the case of Christianityand Islam where slavery was accepted. With the secularisation of industrial capitalist societies,religious inequality became less significant socially. But it brought in racial and economic inequalityjustified in the name of 'Social Darwinism' which gave a special significance to the notion of'survival of the fittest'.

Thirdly, the classical political economy of modern capitalism and utilitarianism also justified inequality. This view of economic struggle is associated with the notion of possessive individualism,achievement and initiative. The economic doctrine of inequality associated with utilitarianism isfundamental to the general culture of capitalist society. It is difficult to distinguish betweenpolitical theories of inequality and the classical economic analysis of inequality arising from themarket place.

Apart from the above, there are many common arguments against equality.

Firstly, it is argued that there are different components of equality which are mutually incompatible.

Secondly, the political programmes of equality are not feasible.

Thirdly, equality is not desirable since achievement ofequality may be incompatible with other values which are also desirable such as liberty.

Fourthly, the functional theory of stratification believes that there are some social positions which significantly contribute to the maintenance and continuation of the whole social system.

Fifthly, it is suggested that inequality in economic terms has a number of important socialfunctions both for society and for specific social groups.

Finally, inequalities of wealth are important in subsidising the living standards of upper and middleclasses by making their lives more comfortable and enjoyable.

❑ PAST 8 ATTEMPTS IGNOU QUESTIONS

June 2020: Discuss the inter-relationship of equality with liberty and justice.

Answer by India Ebook: Exact same as **Q.3** of the Above.

6. MPS-001: UNIT-6: Justice

- ➢ Introduction
- ➢ The Idea of Justice – Procedural & Substantive
- ➢ Rawls' Liberal-Egalitarian Principles of Social Justice
    - ✦ Critique of Utilitarianism
    - ✦ Rawls' Liberal-Egalitarian Principles of Justice
    - ✦ The Social Contract Procedure
    - ✦ The Basic Structure of Society
- ➢ Some Criticisms of Rawls' Concept of Justice
    - ✦ The Libertarian Critique
    - ✦ Some Marxist Criticisms
    - ✦ The Communitarian Critique

IGNOU Book Exercise & Past 8 Attempts Questions - IMPORTANT

❑ IGNOU BOOK EXERCISE

2. Critically examine Rawls's egalitarian conception of social justice.

Answer by India Ebook: Rawls's principles of social justice are a corrective to the liberal-utilitarian principle of the greatest happiness of the greatest number. <u>What then are his objections to utilitarianism</u>?

Rawls recognises that liberal utilitarianism marked a progressive, welfare-oriented departure from classical liberalism's preoccupation with individualistic rights. Yet, utilitarianism is, in Rawls's view, a morally flawed theory of justice. Its moral flaw is that it justifies or condones the sacrificing of the good of some individuals for the sake of the happiness of the greatest number. For the utilitarians, the criterion of justice in a society is the aggregate sum of utility or happiness or welfare it produces, and not the well-being or welfare of each member of the society.

❑ **Rawls's Liberal-Egalitarian Principles of Justice**

❖ **Principle 1 (Principle of Equal Basic Liberties)**

Each person has the same indefeasible claim to a fully adequate scheme of equal basic liberties, scheme which is compatible with the same scheme of liberties for all.

❖ **Principle 2**

(2-i: Fair Equality of Opportunity; 2-ii: Difference Principle)

Social and economic inequalities are to satisfy two conditions : first, they are to be attached to offices and positions open to all under conditions of fair equality of opportunity; and second, they are to be to the greatest benefit of the least-advantaged members of society

❑ **The Social Contract Procedure**

So far, our focus has been on the content or substance of Rawls's principles of social/distributive justice. Let us now turn briefly to his method or procedure of argumentation in defense of those principles. Why, according to Rawls, should we accept his principles, rather than some other principles (say, the utilitarian or libertarian principles), as principles of just or fair distribution?

Briefly stated, Rawls's response is that a social contract method or procedure of political deliberation respects the Kantian liberal-egalitarian moral idea of the freedom and equality of all persons and that an agreement or contract arrived at through such a method or procedure is just or fair to all the parties to that contract. He, in fact, adopts such a procedure and argues that all the contractors would agree to the above-mentioned general and special formulations of the principles of distributive justice – principles, which he espouses and defends as the liberal democratic-egalitarian principles of social justice.

❑ **The Basic Structure of Society**

Rawls has persuasively shown that social justice is of crucial importance to social life and that it should inform constitutions, laws, policies, legal processes, etc. In fact, according to him, the primary subject of justice is the basic structure of society. His principles of social justice justifies, and is justified by, liberal democracy, a regulated market economy and the liberal-egalitarian welfare state.

He states that for translating his Difference Principle into practice, the government should have **four branches**, viz.,

i) an allocation branch "to keep the price system workably competitive and to prevent the formation of unreasonable market power"

ii) a stabilization branch to bring about "reasonably full employment" and, jointly with the allocation branch, to maintain the efficiency of the market economy

iii) a transfer branch to attend to "the claims of need and an appropriate standard of life" and

iv) a distribution branch "to preserve an appropriate justice in distributive shares" by taxation measures and adjustments in property rights.

❑ PAST 8 ATTEMPTS IGNOU QUESTIONS

June 2022: Critically examine John Rawl's theory of Justice.

Answer by India Ebook: Almost same as **Q.2** of the Above.

June 2021: Examine Rawl's conception of Justice.

Answer by India Ebook: Almost same as **Q.2** of the Above.

June 2020: Attempt a critique of John Rawl's theory of Justice.

Answer by India Ebook: Almost same as **Q.2** of the Above.

7. MPS-001: UNIT-7: Idea of Duty

- Introduction
- Significance of Duty
- Meaning
- Duties & Rights
  - Distinct Spaces of Duties and Rights within Liberal Thought - (i) Interest Theory, (ii) Choice Theory, (iii) Autonomy, (iv) Justice
  - Duties and Rights in the Conservative Perspective
  - Duties and Rights in the Communitarian Perspective
  - Duties and Rights in the Gandian Perspective
- Types of Duties

IGNOU Book Exercise & Past 8 Attempts Questions - IMPORTANT

- ❏ **IGNOU BOOK EXERCISE**
- ❏ **PAST 8 ATTEMPTS IGNOU QUESTIONS**

June 2022: Examine the inter-relationship of duties and rights.

Answer by India Ebook: **Duties are** closely associated <u>with rights in liberal thought.</u> The nature and degree of this association, however, has greatly differed. In **pre-liberal societies** where persons were caught in social roles, and people were not free to pursue their choices, duties ordered their lives.

Liberal transportation led to stress on rights and duties were seen as correlated to rights. If a person possessed rights, then others – be **it individuals, groups or the state** as the case may be, were invested with a determinate set of duties to protect and promote those rights.

If I have a right to physical security, others have a duty <u>not to violate or assault </u>such security and if it was violated or assaulted, the state is duty bound to come to my protection.

This correspondence between rights and duties which led to the effective collapsing of duties within rights has been challenged from within liberal thought as well as from outside its framework.

Within the liberal tradition, broadly defined as invoking centrality of rights, we can identify five distinct positions with respect to the relation of duties and rights.

❑ Interest Theory

This theory was initially stated by **Jeremy Bentham** who saw rights not as natural or moral, but as products of law. He argued that the law by creating duties stipulates rights. He said, *"It makes me liable to punishment in case of my doing any of those acts which would have the effects of disturbing you in the exercise of that right (Hart, 1978)."* There is no right if there is no corresponding duty sanctioned by law.

This understanding of the relation is sometimes called as 'sanction theory'. It makes possession of a right as another's legal duty and it becomes a legal duty only if it is liable for punishment.

This way of constructing duties need not preclude social sanctions of a kind. Individuals as members of non-state organisations may be subject to rules and to the imposition of sanctions, if they break those rules.

❑ Choice Theory

The choice or will theory counter poses itself against the interest theory stipulating the relation between rights and duties. One of the important proponents of this theory is **H.L.A. Hart**. He suggested that a right is a form of choice.

The essential feature of a right is that the person to whom the duty is owed is able to control the performance of that duty. The duty-right relation is a chain which binds one individual, the bearer of the duty, and whose other end is in the hands of another individual, the bearer of the right to use it according to his will. It could beget the following relations:

(a) The right holder may waive or extinguish the duty or leave it in existence.

(b) After a breach or threatened breach of a duty, the right holder may leave the duty unforced or may reinforce it by suing for compensation.

(c) The right holder may waive or extinguish the obligation to pay compensation resulting from the breach of duty.

❑ Autonomy

Autonomy is the *capacity for reflection and to formulate* and **revise our preferences, desires, values** and **ideas**. The philosopher **Immanuel Kant** advanced a theoretical formulation of this notion and put forward a specific conception of duty in relation to this capacity.

He **suggested** that the behaviour of the non-human world is governed by nature. Non-human beings did not will to act, but acted subject to natural forces and instinct.

❑ Justice

John Rawls proposes a set of principles to inform a just society which, he argues, all reasonable people will concur. These **principles establish a fair and equal** basis for collective life expressed in terms of rights.

These principles of justice **lead to two sorts of principles**: Principles for institutions which apply to the basic structure of society, and principles for individuals which set the duties **and** obligations of persons with respect to institutions and one another.

For **Rawls**, persons are bound to abide by social practices upholding a just society on the basis of natural duty or obligation. He, therefore, makes the distinction between **duty and obligations.**

Dec 2019: What is the Gandhian perspective on duties and rights? Explain.

Answer by India Ebook: A duty generally prescribes what **we ought to do** and **what we ought not do**. It is a reason for action. Duty specifies the terms that are binding on individuals and groups in their social practices.

It has been suggested that our conscious practices can be seen as motivated by **right-based, duty-based or goal-based perspectives** (Dworkin, 1978 and Weldron, 1984).

While **our practices might be governed by all these perspectives**, one of them might be fundamental. A duty-based perspective appeals to duty and the reasons embedded therein to uphold and justify our practices.

Duty-based propositions **need not deny rights or satisfactions** that the other two perspectives suggest, but they necessarily assert the priority of the former over the latter as in an argument of the kind below: *"A citizen should vote and participate in shaping and forming public life. His civic and political rights must depend upon the extent to which he participates in public life. He cannot demand rewards and benefits from public life unless he has extended such support and participation".*

M.K. Gandhi is well known for his stress on duties and his identification of dharma as the path of duty. He also upheld the values of **'swaraj'**, i.e. self-rule. Such a fusion of dharma and swaraj, or **duty and freedom**, is a characteristic mark of Gandhian thought.

Gandhi argues that all **men and women are equal**. The doctrine of **advaita** upholds it. "If I am That and besides That there is none else", being characteristic of **advaita**, every being has to be regarded as supreme.

Swaraj for Gandhi is a pursuit within the reach of everyone. It involves the duty of self-discipline and a transformation on that basis.

At the same time, **Gandhi opposed domination**. He held that **freedom is necessary for moral growth**.

For Gandhi, *equality is one of the greatest* good to be cherished. Other goods like **dignity and integrity** were closely interwoven with it. **Gandhi rejected considerations** such as gender, birth, class, caste, education and nationality as justifying unequal treatment.

At the same time, Gandhi upheld the **path of dharma** and he considered the **Varnashrama dharma** as the appropriate path of duty.

He argued that **varna** set human-beings free for extending the field of spiritual research&spiritual evolution.

8. MPS-001: UNIT-8: Citizenship

- Introduction and Significance; Nature of Citizenship
- Liberal Democracy, Citizenship & Civic Culture
- Marxism and Citizenship
- Persons and Citizenship
- Group-Differentiated Citizenship
  - ❖ Citizenship as an Attribute Independent of Cultural Identity
  - ❖ Citizenship as a Group Differentiated Identity

IGNOU Book Exercise & Past 8 Attempts Questions – IMPORTANT

❑ IGNOU BOOK EXERCISE

1. Explain the natural significance of citizenship in democratic societies.

Answer by India Ebook: Citizenship is a relationship between an individual and a state to which the individual owes allegiance and in turn is entitled to its protection.

Each **state determines the conditions** under which it will recognize persons as its citizens, and the conditions under which that status will be withdrawn. Recognition by a state as a citizen generally carries with it recognition of civil, political, and social rights which are not afforded to non-citizens.

In general, the basic rights normally regarded as arising from citizenship are the right to a passport, the right to leave and return to the country/ies of citizenship, the right to live in that country, and to work there.

Some **countries permit** their citizens to have multiple citizenships, while others insist on exclusive allegiance.

The **growing significance** of citizenship has not put to rest the **theoretical ambiguity** associated with this notion. The importance of the **concept of citizenship** to engage with a series of political processes and values and therefore, as a major normative and explanatory variable has undergone significant changes over time.

There was no significant discussion on citizenship in social science literature in the recent past. However, in the last decade and a half, citizenship has suddenly emerged as a central theme in social science literature, both as a normative consideration and social phenomenon. Certain recent trends in the world and in India have increasingly suggested citizenship as a nodal concern.

Overall, there is **greater appreciation** today of the qualities and attitudes of citizens for the health and stability of modern democracy. While increasingly certain rights are **conceded to all human beings in normal times** by states, citizens have certain specific rights which non-citizens do not possess. Most states do not grant the right to vote and to stand for public office to aliens. The same can be said about obligations too.

Just the fact that one is a citizen gives access to many rights which aliens do not enjoy. Aliens become naturalised as citizens with attendant rights and obligations. **Citizenship** can be divided into **three dimensions**:

5. Discuss the relationship between citizenship and cultural identity.

Answer by India Ebook: Group differentiated citizenship qualifies citizenship by cultural belonging. It sees citizenship as constituted of both equal rights and differences. A society avowing group differentiated citizenship appreciates the cultural differences in which equal and free citizens are anchored.

Cultures are modes of life which are much more enduring. While there are instances of people making a successful transition from one culture to another, this is not a reasonable option for a vast number of people. Of course, cultures are not sterile waters. They do undergo significant changes over time, but across these changes they remain the self-same cultures.

Two types of **relationships** are suggested between citizenship and its cultural embeddment.

- ❑ Citizenship as an attribute independent of cultural identity.
- ❑ Citizenship as a group-differentiated identity.

Citizenship As An Attribute Independent of Cultural Identity

Cultural identities constituted as communities uphold moral ideals that are supposed to hold good to all its members. Often they propose a comprehensive way of life which is supposed to be the embodiment of what good life should be for one and all.

It revolves around certain definitive conceptions of what is important and what is not important in life with regard to such fundamental issues such as sex, friendship, work, suffering, sin, death and salvation. It provides definitive order and meaning to such issues. It ranks human qualities and orders aspirations in terms of a hierarchy of ends.

Communities assign stable and well known duties and responsibilities. There are unambiguous standards to evaluate conduct. Communities orient human desire to definitive channels.

Communication in such communities acquires clarity and effectiveness due to sharing in common a range of background assumptions. Communities do not entertain questions on meaning, purpose, value and responsibility on a whole range of activities they are constituted of.

❏ PAST 8 ATTEMPTS IGNOU QUESTIONS

June 2020: Write an essay on Group Differentiated Citizenship.

Answer by India Ebook: Group differentiated citizenship qualifies citizenship by cultural belonging. It sees citizenship as constituted of both equal rights and differences. A society avowing group differentiated citizenship appreciates the cultural differences in which equal and free citizens are anchored.

Cultures are modes of life which are much more enduring. While there are instances of people making a successful transition from one culture to another, this is not a reasonable option for a vast number of people. Of course, cultures are not sterile waters. They do undergo significant changes over time, but across these changes they remain the self-same cultures.

Two types of **relationships** are suggested between citizenship and its cultural embeddment.

- ❏ Citizenship as an attribute independent of cultural identity.
- ❏ Citizenship as a group-differentiated identity.

Citizenship as a Group-Differentiated Identity

In this conception, citizenship means very different things to different communities. The rights that different communities enjoy and the obligations they are expected to shoulder differ, although the principles on which they are grounded are the same. These principles are the significance of community for the constitution of the self and the need to ensure political stability under conditions of freedom and equality.

Three types of rights are suggested under a differentiated understanding of citizenship, although it is possible to suggest a much more complex typology in this regard, considering the kind of deep diversity that prevails in countries like India, Russia, Indonesia and China.

- Citizenship based on Polyethnic Rights
- Special Representation Rights
- Self-Government Rights

NOTES

9. MPS-001: UNIT-9: Sovereignty

- Introduction
- What is Sovereignty?– Definitions & Meaning
- Development of the Concept of Sovereignty
- Kinds of Sovereignty: Real & Titular Sovereignty; Legal & Political Sovereignty; Dejure & Defacto Sovereignty; Concept of Popular Sovereignty
- Austin's Concept of Sovereignty
- Pluralistic Attack on Austin's Concept of Sovereignty
- Sovereignty and Globalization-New Challenges: Sovereignty and Power-Blocs; Sovereignty and Global Economy; Sovereignty and International Organisations; Sovereignty and International Law

IGNOU Book Exercise & Past 8 Attempts Questions - IMPORTANT

- ❑ **IGNOU BOOK EXERCISE**
- ❑ **PAST 8 ATTEMPTS IGNOU QUESTIONS**

Dec 2020: Define Sovereignty and differentiate between Real and Titular Sovereignty.

Answer by India Ebook: Sovereignty is a key concept in traditional political theory. It constitutes one of the **four elements** of the state without which statehood remains incomplete.

Derived from the Latin term Superanus, which means supreme, sovereignty denotes the supreme power of the state to extract obedience from the people who inhabit it.

- ❑ **Sovereignty is "the supreme power over citizens and subjects unrestrained by law". – Bodin**

- ❑ Sovereignty is"the supreme political power vested in him whose acts are not subject to any other and whose will cannot be overridden"
  – Grotius

Internally, the state is supreme to any individual or organisation, living or functioning, within its boundaries, and they have to function under the laws and command of the state. None can claim superiority over or immunity to the state. The power of the state over them is original, total, unlimited and all comprehensive.

Sovereignty also has an **external connotation**, which means that in the comity of states, every state is supreme and is free to cast its destiny. No other state or any international organisation can claim superiority to a state. The state may be subjected to certain treaties or other obligations, but they are self-imposed obligations on the part of the state. None can compel or enforce any obligation on the state, which it is not willing to accept.

Thus, the state is equipped with internal and external sovereignty that gives it over-riding powers over individuals, groups and organisations and makes it absolute.

The term sovereignty has been used in many ways in Political Science that makes its comprehension very difficult. Therefore, it is necessary to understand its varied uses.

REAL & TITULAR SOVEREIGNTY

Initially, the king was all powerful and actually exercised his powers. But with the development of democracy, the king was devoid of his powers and the parliament became supreme. However, the English people loved monarchy and did not abolish it. Instead, the powers of the king were transferred to an institution called the Crown.

The monarchy in England still exists and all the powers are exercised in the name of the king or the queen but the real sovereign is the Crown. This distinction also exists in countries where the parliamentary form of government is prevalent.

Like in India, where the president is the titular head while the real sovereign is the prime minister and his cabinet. In a country like the USA, no such distinction exists as the president is said to be both real as well as the titular sovereign.

Dec 2018: Explain the pluralists critique of John Austin's concept of sovereignty.

Answer by India Ebook: Sovereignty is the **supreme power** of the state by which the state exerts its authority. Legally speaking, there cannot be any restriction to its power of exerting obedience.

It also monopolises the power of using legitimate physical force. This view is **best represented in Austin's concept of sovereignty** in which sovereignty has been depicted as permanent, absolute, universal, inalienable, exclusive and indivisible.

The pluralist attack on Austin's concept of sovereignty with special reference to Laski and MacIver:

The pluralists **do not believe** that the **sovereign is determinate**. According to them, the determination was possible in old days when the king ruled with absolute powers.

But in modern times the political system is based upon the concept of popular sovereignty in which the government is responsible to the people who can make or unmake the government.

The constitutions clearly proclaim the sovereignty of the people, but Austin will not accept people as sovereign.

The pluralists have remarkably projected this view where they conceived state as an association. They argued for a limited state and division of sovereign powers between the state and other associations.

Though legally the **pluralistic views cannot be acceptable**, politically and socially they are very attractive since they depict modern democratic ideals.

Austin's concept of absolute sovereignty has also been **criticised by the pluralists** on the basis of dangers that it poses to the maintenance of international peace and tranquility. The Pluralists point out that the doctrine of absolute sovereignty is incompatible with the interests of humanity as it leads to destructive wars.

It is also a fact that time is changing very rapidly and theoretically the concept of state sovereignty still exists but very important in-roads have been made especially since globalisation has curtailed the effectiveness of the state supreme power.

10. MPS-001: UNIT-10: State and Civil Society

- ➢ Introduction; State & Civil Society: Meaning & Characteristics
- ➢ Concept of the State: An Overview
  - *The Pre-Modern Tradition, Liberal-Individualist Tradition, The Marxian Tradition*
- ➢ Concept of Civil Society: An Overview
  - *The Pre-Modern Tradition, Liberal-Individualist Tradition, Hegelian Marxian& Gramsian Tradition*
- ➢ Relationship between State & Civil Society
  - *Integrative Relationship, State, Civil Society & Democ*

IGNOU Book Exercise & Past 8 Attempts Questions - IMPORTANT

❑ **IGNOU BOOK EXERCISE**

1. How did the term 'state' come to be used in the West? Explain briefly the characteristic features of State.

Suggeseted Answer by INDIA EBOOK: The term 'state' come to be used in West i.e. Europe in 16th century. The concept of state occupies a **central place** in Political Science. **No discussion** on political theory **is complete** without reference to the word **'state'.** The state, indeed, touches every aspect of human life, and this is why it has, very rightly, captured the attention of all political philosophers since the days of Plato.

The concept of state occupies a **central place** in Political Science. **No discussion** on political theory **is complete** without reference to the word **'state'.**

To understand the state **as an administrative machinery** ordering public life is to know its one aspect. Important though this aspect is, it is not the only aspect which explains as to what it is. The state is where it operates on.

Its **real meaning** together with its other related implications emerges more clearly when it is understood in relation to the **domain of its area of operation**, which is what society is.

State is not mere governance; it is a political community as well. The state, as a **word stato**, appeared in **Italy** in the early part of the sixteenth century in the **writings of Machiavelli** (1469-1527).

State exists within the society. This makes the state and society analytically distinct. The two are not the same. Society is a web of social relationships and as such, includes the totality of social practices, which are essentially plural, but at the same time, are relational. The state, as a social relation and also as a codified power in a given society, would have certain characteristics of its own. **These characteristics can be stated as:**

a) The state is a power, organised in itself. It has the power to legitimise social relations and gives them recognition through formal codes and institutions. This gives the state a distinct and irreducible status in society while making it autonomous from classes and contending factions existing in it.

b) The state emerges as a set of specifically political practices which defines binding decisions and enforces them, to the extent of intervening in every aspect of social life.

c) The state monopolises all means of coercion. No other organisation in the society has this power.

d) The state gives fixity to social relations, and social stability to society.

e) The state exists within the framework of a given society. As society responds to the changing conditions compelled by numerous social forces, the state responds to the changing society. The state always reflects the changing relations of society. As society constantly re-enacts itself, so does the state.

The liberal and the marxist perspectives of civil society **differ drastically.**

For the **liberals**, civil society presupposes democratic states together with the accountability of the states, the limits on state power, the responsiveness to the spontaneous life and the interactions of civil society.

For the **marxists**, civil society is the arena of class conflicts, selfish competition and exploitation, the state acting to protect the interests of the owning classes.

5. What is civil society? Explain **Hegel's view** of civil society.

Suggeseted Answer by INDIA EBOOK: **Civil society** consists of the entire range of assumptions, values and institutions such as political, social and civil rights, the rule of law, representative institutions, a public sphere and above all, a plurality of associations. The liberal and the marxist perspectives of civil society **differ drastically.**

For the **liberals**, civil society presupposes democratic states together with the accountability of the states, the limits on state power, the responsiveness to the spontaneous life and the interactions of civil society.

For the **marxists**, civil society is the arena of class conflicts, selfish competition and exploitation, the state acting to protect the interests of the owning classes.

A definition of civil society comprising the insights of both liberals & marxists must take into account following:

a) The state power must be controlled and it has to become responsive through democratic practices of an independent civil society.

b) Political accountability has to reside not only in constitutions, laws, and regulations, but also in the social fabric or what Habermas calls the competence of the '**political public**' which, in turn, has the following implications:

(i)   it implies that the people come together in an arena of common concerns, in debates & discussion & discourse free from state interference

(ii)   it implies that the discourse is accessible to all

(iii)   it implies a space where public discussion and debate can take place.

c) Democratic norms and processes have to be imbibed in the social order.

d) Civil society is the public sphere of society. It is the location of these processes by which the experiences of individuals and communities, and the expression of experiences in debates and discussions, affirmation and constitution are mediated.

In the writings of **Hegel** there is a definite relationship between the **state and civil society**. The concept of civil society is associated with the Western intellectual tradition. With the epoichal changes in the West, the idea of civil society has grown progressively. Many factors have gone into developing the concept of the state as it has come to stay with us.

These factors, to mention a few, include the emergence of secular authority, the development of the institution of property, the decline of the absolutist state, the growth of urban culture, the rise of nationalist and democratic movements, until the end of the nineteenth century and the rule of law. As the capitalist economy with its democratising features has developed, so has the concept of civil society.

There is a definite relationship between the state and civil society in the writings of **Hegel** (1770-1831). He views the state as the latest link growing out of the development of various institutions. Describing the state as the synthesis, representing universality, of the thesis of families and the anti-thesis of civil society, Hegel recognises the state as higher in kind than civil society. Hegel regards the state as the highest, the latest, and even the final form of social institutions.

6. Explain the relationship between state and civil society.

Suggeseted Answer by INDIA EBOOK: **State** is not mere governance; it is a political community as well. The state, as a word stato, appeared in Italy in the early part of the sixteenth century in the writings of Machiavelli (1469-1527).

It is, what **Gramsci** says, the visible political constitution of civil society, consisting of the entire complex of activities with which a ruling class maintains its dominance, and the ways in which it manages to win the consent of those over which it rules.

It is, **in other words**, a complex of institutions and practices resting upon the nodal points of power in civil society. It is a social relation and as such, it is the codified power of social formation. **Civil society** consists of the entire range of assumptions, values and institutions such as political, social and civil rights, the rule of law, representative institutions, a public sphere and above all, a plurality of associations.

The relationship between state and civil society is important in so far as it suggests the comparative position of each in relation to the other. In some analyses, this relationship is depicted as a zerosum game: the stronger the state, the weaker the civil society; the weaker the state, the stronger the civil society.

❑ State and Civil Society: Integrative Relationship

State and civil society are **not two opposite concepts**. One does not stand in conflict with another. Neither is one the anti-thesis of the other. The two should not be regarded as usurping the area of each other. It is not a zero-sum game relationship between the two. Indeed, the relatively stronger state would put a premium on the role of civil society, but this, in no way, diminishes the effectiveness of civil society.

The **integrative framework**, as expressed in laws and rules, is accepted as valid by all, the framework needs to be administered neutrally and in a manner consistent with the shared culture of society. We cannot imagine life without this integrative framework, which creates a degree of coherence and without which civil society is likely to become uncivil. Civil society has to open up, in the face of the all-powerful state, to challenge the bureaucratic devices lest it ends up in rigidity. It is, thus, the reciprocity between state and civil society that is significant or at least, should be considered significant. State power is to be exercised within the larger and wider sphere of civil society, and civil society has to keep state power on its toes so that it does not degenerate into absolutism.

7. How does democracy ensure an integrative relationship between the state and the civil society?

Suggeseted Answer by INDIA EBOOK: **State** is not mere governance; it is a political community as well. The state, as a word stato, appeared in Italy in the early part of the sixteenth century in the writings of Machiavelli (1469-1527).

It is, what **Gramsci** says, the visible political constitution of civil society, consisting of the entire complex of activities with which a ruling class maintains its dominance, and the ways in which it manages to win the consent of those over which it rules.

It is, **in other words**, a complex of institutions and practices resting upon the nodal points of power in civil society. It is a social relation and as such, it is the codified power of social formation. **Civil society** consists of the entire range of assumptions, values and institutions such as political, social and civil rights, the rule of law, representative institutions, a public sphere and above all, a plurality of associations.

RELATIONSHIP BETWEEN STATE AND CIVIL SOCIETY

The relationship between state and civil society is important in so far as it suggests the comparative position of each in relation to the other. In some analyses, this relationship is depicted as a zerosum game: the stronger the state, the weaker the civil society; the weaker the state, the stronger the civil society.

STATE, CIVIL SOCIETY AND DEMOCRACY

The two concepts, state and civil society, are not in conflict with each other. Democracy integrates the two. The claims of the state get strengthened by civil society and civil society is made more stable through the state. The two have to work in a democratic frame: the democratic state within the framework of democratic civil society.

Civil society has to be more open and diversified. It has to keep the dialogue continuous and constant with the state and within all the constituents making it. Its area has to be ordained freely and openly, devices making up public opinion and public discourse state-free.

A democratic state cannot exist if it is restrictive, coercive, prohibitive, and imposing; it cannot exist if it does not provide the civil society frame in perfect order; it cannot exist if it does not guarantee rights and freedoms to individuals.

The state, in democratic systems, protects civil society and civil society strengthens the state. In dictatorial regimes, the state controls the civil society.

❑ PAST 8 ATTEMPTS IGNOU QUESTIONS

No Questions asked in last 8 attempts.

11. MPS-001: UNIT-11: Power and Authority

> Introduction; Empirical Study of Power; Concept of Power; Power – Marxist and Western Approach

> Concept of Authority; Development of the Concept of Authority

IGNOU Book Exercise & Past 8 Attempts Questions - IMPORTANT

❑ IGNOU BOOK EXERCISE

1. Explain the concept of power and its various dimensions.

Suggeseted Answer by INDIA EBOOK: The concept of power is the key to understand and analyse politics, political institutions and political movements of the systemic process, both in the national and international arena. It is the centre of political theory. While studying the concept of power and its various manifestations in the systemic processes, one is reminded of what.

CONCEPTS OF POWER: Power is normally understood as the possession of control, authority, or influence over others, a relationship in which an individual or a group is able to exert influence over the minds and actions of others.

Most of the researchers who analyse the concept of power often start with two propositions: that in any polity some people have more powers than others, and that power is an object of desire, a 'utility'. Power is understandably associated with honour, deference, respect and dignity. One has, of course, to distinguish the power of the man from the power of the office that guarantees authority and legitimacy.

One has also to be careful about the distinction between apparent and real power. While analysing various dimensions of power, **Maslow** prefers to talk about the psycho –pathology of ambition as well as mental framework of some men.

DIMENSIONS OF POWER: One of **Lukes'** academic theories is that of the **"three faces of power,"** presented in his book, Power: A Radical View. This theory claims that power is exercised in three ways: decision-making power, non-decision-making power, and ideological power.

Decision-making power is the most public of the three dimensions. Analysis of this "face" focuses on policy preferences revealed through political action.

Non-decision-making power is that which sets the agenda in debates and makes certain issues (e.g., the merits of socialism in the United States) unacceptable for discussion in "legitimate" public forums. Adding this face gives a two-dimensional view of power allowing the analyst to examine both current and potential issues, expanding the focus on observable conflict to those types that might be observed overtly or covertly.

Ideological power allows one to influence people's wishes and thoughts, even making them want things opposed to their own self-interest (e.g., causing women to support a patriarchal society). Lukes offers this third dimension as a "thoroughgoing critique" of the behavioural focus of the first two dimensions, supplementing and correcting the shortcomings of previous views, allowing the analyst to include both latent and observable conflicts. Lukes claims that a full critique of power should include both subjective interests and those "real" interests held by those excluded by the political process.

2. Discuss the Marxist and western views of the concept of power.

Suggeseted Answer by INDIA EBOOK: The concept of power is the key to understand and analyse politics, political institutions and political movements of the systemic process, both in the national and international arena. It is the centre of political theory. While studying the concept of power and its various manifestations in the systemic processes, one is reminded of what.

POWER – MARXIST AND WESTERN APPROACH

a. The concept of power is one of the fundamental concepts of political theory. The analysis of the nature of power in both socialist and capitalist societies is essential for understanding the nature of politics as well as the state.

b. **Lenin** said, " The question of power cannot be evaded or brushed aside, because it is the key question determining everything in a revolution's development, and in its foreign and domestic politics".

c. While studying the concept of power, what often comes to mind is its use in a broad sense by the Marxist thinkers. Both Marx and Lenin highlighted the social relations in a political system as well as the relationship between man and environment.

d. With the control of man over nature because of growth in science and technology, the concept of power acquired a new definition and dimension. As a synonym of political and social domination in state structures, power assumed multi-dimensional forms.

e. In the Marxist approach and terminology, the concept of power is identified with the control of state power through revolutions.

f. According to the Marxist thinkers, the sphere of politics includes all aspects of the state; it implies all types of relationship among the classes, be it economic, ideological, semi-psychological and other. Lenin said, "it is the sphere of relationships of all classes and strata to the state and the government, the sphere of interaction between all classes."

g. The western sociologist highlights power as an essential factor in all social kinetics. The French sociologist talks of "the aura of mystery surrounding power".

h. Some of the western thinkers have also talked about the biological concept of power. Going back to the Greek days, Aristotle viewed power as a natural condition of society, nature determining the character and process of society.

i. Some of the leading western sociologists were not in favour of this tendency towards biologism. George Burdeau, for example emphasised that power and society were born together.

j. Some researchers like Herbert Simon have presented a very narrow definition of power. Simon uses the concepts of power and influence as synonyms.

k. The western concept of power as the capacity to work one's will is reflected in the writings of Engels when he said, "Authority, in the sense in which the word is used here, means the imposition of the will of another upon ours; on the other hand, authority presupposes subordination."

l. Thus, both western political sociology and Marxist thinking on the growth of political systems have contributed a great deal towards the development of the concept of power.

3. Explain the difference between power and authority.

Suggeseted Answer by INDIA EBOOK: **Power** is normally understood as the possession of control, authority, or influence over others, a relationship in which an individual or a group is able to exert influence over the minds and actions of others.

Most of the researchers who analyse the concept of power often start with two propositions: that in any polity some people have more powers than others, and that power is an object of desire, a 'utility'. Power is understandably associated with honour, deference, respect and dignity. One has, of course, to distinguish the power of the man from the power of the office that guarantees authority and legitimacy.

One has also to be careful about the distinction between apparent and real power. While analysing various dimensions of power, **Maslow** prefers to talk about the psycho –pathology of ambition as well as mental framework of some men.

DIMENSIONS OF POWER

One of **Lukes'** academic theories is that of the **"three faces of power,"** presented in his book, Power: A Radical View. This theory claims that power is exercised in **three** ways:

> Decision-making power,
> Non-decision-making power, and
> Ideological power.

Authority is broadly understood as a constitutional means through which one can command compliance or obedience and influence the behaviour of another. Whereas power is broadly concerned with the ability to influence behaviour, 'authority' is understood as the right to do so. Political philosophers over the decades have differed regarding the fundamental basis on which authority rested.

Authority provokes deep political and ideological disagreements. Some regard it as essential to the maintenance of an ordered, stable and healthy society, providing individuals with clear guidance and support. Others warn that authority tends to be the enemy of liberty and undermines reason and moral responsibility; authority tends to lead to authoritarianism.

Modern sociologists have approached the concept of authority from a different angle. The German sociologist, Max Weber, considers authority as a form of power, a 'legitimate power'.

AUTHORITY VS. POWER

Basically, both power and authority are mutually exclusive concepts. Authority is widely understood as a means of gaining compliance. On the other hand, power involves the ability to accomplish goals. It might take various forms such as pressure, intimidation, coercion or violence. Authority and power are intrinsically interlinked.

Authority is rarely exercised in the absence of power, and power always implies some amount of authority.

Some **points of differences** between **Power and Authority** are tabled below:

Power	Authority
Is the ability to exert one's will. It is a personal ability to influence others or events.	Is a formal right given to take decisions and give direction (commands) based on agreed parameters.
Is based on a combination of knowledge, expertise, social skills, emotional intelligence and the ability to influence others.	Is based on the formal rights given to a position and rank within an organisation.
The scope of power is determined by the individual wielding it.	The scope of authority is agreed, explicit and can be written down.
Power can flow in any direction, it is not linked to a hierarchy. Individuals can influence their boss and peers. It has horizontal and vertical flow.	Authority flows down through an organisation's hierarchy, from the top down.

❑ PAST 8 ATTEMPTS IGNOU QUESTIONS

June 2019: 1. Explain the concept of Power and its various dimensions.

Suggeseted Answer by INDIA EBOOK: Exact Same Answer as above **Q. No 1.**

12. MPS-001: UNIT-12: Legitimation and Obligation

- ➢ Introduction
- ➢ What is Legitimation?
  - ⁺ Legitimation & the State; Legitimation & Legitimacy; Power, Legitimation and Authority
- ➢ What is Obligation?
  - ⁺ Types of Obligation: Moral & Legal; Duty, Obligation & Conflict
  - ⁺ Concept of Political Obligation
- ➢ Why Obey the Government? An Overview
  - ⁺ L & O – Basis of Paternalism, Basis of Contract, Basis of Consent
- ➢ Legitimation and Obligation Crises
  - ⁺ Overloaded Government Theory, The Legitimation Crisis Theory – Analyzed

IGNOU Book Exercise & Past 8 Attempts Questions - IMPORTANT

❑ **IGNOU BOOK EXERCISE**

1. What do you mean by legitimation?

Suggeseted Answer by INDIA EBOOK: **Legitimation** amounts to pronouncing what is lawful, i.e., what is in accordance with established rules, principles or standards? It is what is related to the laws and decrees of the state, sovereign or government. It is what has the sanction of force behind it. It is what is followed, if violated, by punishment.

Legitimacy is the sense of **'rightfulness'** - which makes **authority** different from **power**.

Legitimation is **legalisation**. This means that what is legal is what is legitimate, and conversely what is not legal, i.e., what is not in accordance with law, established rules, recognised norms, is not legitimate. It is in this sense that legitimation is related to what is lawful. Literally, legitimation means, **"to make lawful"**.

Legitimation is, thus, the power of the state rightfully exercised and is the acceptance so by those on whom it exercises its control. So understood, the concept of legitimation includes, if one attempts to identify its inherent implications, in the first instance

(i) the legalised patterns of state activities,

(ii) the value systems of society in which the state exercises control and

(iii) the citizens' body recognises the state's power legitimately-based.

LEGITIMATION AND THE STATE

The state's very **strength** is based on **legitimation**. The structure of power, peculiar to the state, has to be legitimately derived and evolved; the exercise of the power of the state also needs to be used legitimately.

If the **state is to carry** on its business, with at least a minimum amount of consent from its citizens, and if the government is to survive, it requires legitimation/legitimacy. Obviously, without legitimation of state power, the alternative is the use of physical force or terror to enforce the orders of the state. In a democratically structured society, state power is legitimate **when:**

(a) the power to rule the people is given by the people, and is exercised with the consent of the majority of the people – this would mean that those who exercise power are elected directly or indirectly by the people for a limited period only, and also when a system of control is in place

(b) when the state power is exercised corresponding to the principles stated in the constitution of the land, especially those relating to legality.

Legitimation is related to the state in more than one way. It is related to the state in the sense that the state alone has the legal authority to use its power.

Legitimation, in the context of the state, **also demands compliance** from the people where the state exercises its power. When the power of the state is accepted by the people, there is no crisis of legitimation. A crisis of legitimation occurs when the power of the state, exercised as it is, is challenged by the people or a part thereof.

2. Distinguish between legitimation and legitimacy. How are the two concepts related to each other?

Suggeseted Answer by INDIA EBOOK: **Legitimation** amounts to pronouncing what is lawful, i.e., what is in accordance with established rules, principles or standards? It is what is related to the laws and decrees of the state, sovereign or government. It is what has the sanction of force behind it. It is what is followed, if violated, by punishment.

Legitimacy is the Status or Condition which exists when an entity's value system is congruent with that of society.

Legitimation is the process which leads to an organisation being viewed as legitimate.

The state's very **strength** is based on **legitimation**. The structure of power, peculiar to the state, has to be legitimately derived and evolved; the exercise of the power of the state also needs to be used legitimately.

If the **state is to carry** on its business, with at least a minimum amount of consent from its citizens, and if the government is to survive, it requires legitimation/legitimacy. Obviously, without legitimation of state power, the alternative is the use of physical force or terror to enforce the orders of the state. In a democratically structured society, state power is legitimate **when:**

(a) the power to rule the people is given by the people, and is exercised with the consent of the majority of the people – this would mean that those who exercise power are elected directly or indirectly by the people for a limited period only, and also when a system of control is in place

(b) when the state power is exercised corresponding to the principles stated in the constitution of the land, especially those relating to legality.

Legitimation is related to the state in more than one way. It is related to the state in the sense that the state alone has the legal authority to use its power.

Legitimation has much in common with the concept of 'legitimacy'.

Legitimacy appears only if the people accept the state's authority to rule without being forced. It is legitimation that creates legitimacy, and it is legitimacy that induces people to accept the right of the state to rule.

Legitimation and legitimacy are **complementary** to each other. The former makes the ground for the latter while the latter derives its strength from the former.

The **difference** between the **two** is that of importance which is attached to it in relation to power or its exercise by the state. The two concepts work more in association with each other than in opposition to each other.

It is **legitimacy** or **one may say self 'legitimation'** that **turns power into authority**. Power becomes authority only through legitimacy or through the process of legitimation. Power without the process of legitimation becomes arbitrariness or mere force. It is, therefore, legitimacy which converts power into authority. With no legitimation of authority, power becomes a brute force.

The Apartheid regime in **South Africa** during the white minority rule can be cited as an example of **'power regime'** <u>without legitimacy</u>.

There, as is known, a <u>white minority enjoyed all political rights</u>, and their government ruled over the black majority. That government had no legitimate authority in the country, for it lacked legitimacy in the eyes of the vast majority of the people – the **Blacks**.

3. What do you mean by obligation?

Suggeseted Answer by INDIA EBOOK: The **two concepts, legitimation and obligation, are so related** that the former seeks to demand or pursue something while the latter seeks to accept or follow. Legitimation is a matter of seeking obedience, whereas obligation is a matter of accepting dominance.

Legitimation amounts to pronouncing what is lawful, i.e., what is in accordance with established rules, principles or standards? It is what is related to the laws and decrees of the state, sovereign or government. It is what has the sanction of force behind it. It is what is followed, if violated, by punishment.

Obligation is, generally, something by which a person is bound to do certain things; something which arises out of a sense of duty; it is what binds a person to a duty, to obedience. It is, in a sense, a state of being legally indebted.

Obligation means the act of binding oneself, binding oneself to some duty, to some contract, to some promise. It is binding someone to do something. Obviously, it arises out of a sense of duty.

To understand the term **'obligation'** more clearly, it is <u>better to relate </u>the term 'obligation' to **'bound' than to 'owing'.**

We may be **bound to perform some action** without in an obvious sense owing anybody anything. To be 'bound' is not to be in bonds. What at best it means is acceptance of a submission, or say losing a certain amount of freedom.

When we accept submission, we accept to work within certain limitations, and such a submission remains until obligation stays; a certain amount of lost freedom is not regained until the obligation has been discharged.

So understood, the **concept of obligation includes**, if one seeks to identify its inherent implications,

(i) an act of binding oneself to some duty,

(ii) a situation characteristic of a relational relationship,

(iii) an authority, say the government with assured rights over the individuals, and the individuals, agreeing to obeying the laws of such an authority.

TYPES OF OBLIGATIONS: MORAL AND LEGAL

Obligations are **not all alike**. There are obligations of which we are conscious; for instance, not 'being in debt' is an obligation of which we are conscious; 'feeling in debt', on the other hand, is an obligation of which we may not be conscious.

If, for example, a man is obliged by law to pay taxes, the obligation is no less real for his being unaware of it. If a man, to take another example, is liable for military service, he is no less obliged to accept and act upon the call for his being totally unprepared for its coming.

All our legal and political obligations, obviously, are obligations of which we are all aware of.

7. State briefly Habermas's view of

legitimation crisis.

Suggeseted Answer by INDIA EBOOK: **Legitimation and Obligation** are intimately related concepts. Legitimation induces obligation, while obligation strengthens the claims of legitimation. The two concepts have captured the imagination of philosophers from the ancient Greek times onwards.

Political theorists, in every age, have answered questions relating to legitimation and obligation in numerous ways. An attempt to review these questions and arguments supporting them would be both interesting and instructive.

Legitimation amounts to pronouncing what is lawful, i.e., what is in accordance with established rules, principles or standards? It is what is related to the laws and decrees of the state, sovereign or government. It is what has the sanction of force behind it. It is what is followed, if violated, by punishment.

Obligation is, generally, something by which a person is bound to do certain things; something which arises out of a sense of duty; it is what binds a person to a duty, to obedience. It is, in a sense, a state of being legally indebted.

The **two concepts, legitimation and obligation, are so related** that the former seeks to demand or pursue something while the latter seeks to accept or follow. Legitimation is a matter of seeking obedience, whereas obligation is a matter of accepting dominance.

No system is _**free from crisis**_. The crises occur because of one factor or the other. Because of the crises, problems with regard to legitimation and obligation spring up. Legitimacy of the government is put to question and obligation to obey the government comes to be overburdened.

All systems experience **problems of crises** relating to legitimation and obligation. No system, in fact, is free from crises at one time or the other, with one factor or several factors responsible for such crises.

Crises occur, whether they relate to challenging the legitimacy of the government or people's obligation to obey the laws of the state, not because of the casual/accidental changes in the environment, but because of the "structurally inherent systems – imperatives that are incompatible and cannot be hierarchically integrated" (see **Habermas, Legitimation Crisis 1976**).

Referring to the advanced capitalist societies, **Habermas** says that such societies experience **four levels of crises**: economic, rationality, legitimation and motivation crisis.

It is not necessary, Habermas states, that these crises may lead to a revolutionary rupture in the system.

8. Analyse briefly the theory of overloaded government in relation to legitimation and obligation.

Suggeseted Answer by INDIA EBOOK: The theory of overloaded Government is related with Legitimation and Obligation. **Legitimation and Obligation** are intimately related concepts. Legitimation induces obligation, while obligation strengthens the claims of legitimation. The two concepts have captured the imagination of philosophers from the ancient Greek times onwards.

Political theorists, in every age, have answered questions relating to legitimation and obligation in numerous ways. An attempt to review these questions and arguments supporting them would be both interesting and instructive.

a) The overloaded government theorists characterise power relations in terms of fragmentation. According to them, power is shared and bartered by numerous groups representing diverse and competing interests.

b) In a pluralist society, the political outcomes, thus, are determined by democratic processes and pressures, the state attempting to mediate and adjudicate between demands.

c) The economy, following the post-war period, while generating mass affluence and general prosperity owing to booms in consumer goods, new housing, spread of television and entertainment industries, raised expectations in all fields and for all the sections of society.

d) The **politicians & political** parties, in order to **secure maximum votes**, promise more than they can ever deliver, some promising to deliver contradictory, therefore, impossible sets of demands. There is a continuous & constant competition among the political parties, leading ultimately to a spiral of ever-greater promises.

e) The state in pluralist societies proves a failure in providing a firm and effective management. It is unable to arrest inflation, for its public spending processes never stop. Consequently as the state expands, it destroys progressively the realm of individual initiative where the space for free and private enterprise is lost.

f) Democracy, in pluralist societies, becomes only a mechanism, and in the process loses its humanitarian value.

g) The state becomes incapable of managing public affairs effectively; it becomes rather an instrument in the hands of powerful economic organised groups, and in the process, loses its role of providing an impartial and effective administration.

h) The individual becomes sovereign, but only in the rhetorical sense of the term. Freedom becomes a set of liberties without any base of equality.

i) The legitimation of the government, in pluralist societies, causes to be questioned. The obligation on the part of the people to obey the state comes under cloud.

j) A firm and decisive political leadership, among other things, which is less responsive to democratic pressures and demands, may provide solace.

❑ PAST 8 ATTEMPTS IGNOU QUESTIONS

No Questions asked in last 8 attempts.

13. MPS-001: UNIT-13: Cilvil Disobedience and Satyagrah

- Introduction
- Concept of Civil Disobedience
- History of the Concept of Civil Disobedience
- Theory of Civil Disobedience & Existentialist Philosophy
- Gandhian Concept of Civil Disobedience & Satyagraha
- Civil Disobedience in Practice

IGNOU Book Exercise & Past 8 Attempts Questions – IMPORTANT

❑ **IGNOU BOOK EXERCISE**

1. Discuss the importance of satyagraha as a method of conflict resolution.

Suggeseted Answer by INDIA EBOOK: **Mahatma Gandhi** is considered to be the leading theorist in the history of civil disobedience movement. The Gandhian concept of **civil disobedience and satyagraha** is the greatest contribution to mankind in our times.

Gandhi called his concept of civil disobedience as the **doctrine of 'Satyagraha' or 'Truth Force'.** For him, the adjective 'civil' in the phrase ' civil disobedience' referred to peaceful, courteous, and a 'civilised' resistance. To him, the concept of passive resistance is inadequate to grasp the full implications of the concept of 'satyagraha'. He said that one must not only resist passively the injustice and arbitrariness of the government, but also must do so without any feeling of animosity.

Gandhi abandoned the term 'passive resistance', and **chose the term 'satyagraha'.** The concept of satyagraha is devoid of any feelings of hatred and violent means. It is based on spiritual purity. Like Tolstoy, Gandhi was opposed to all forms of violence in his commitments to political actions.

Satyagraha, the **unique** system of **non-violent resistance** to the government's arbitrary methods and actions is, indeed, his **greatest gift to mankind.**

For Gandhi, **Ahimsa** (non-violence) and **Truth** were inseparable. He said that "Ahimsa is the means; Truth is the end." Gandhi used satyagraha as a lever for social movements.

In the concept of 'civil disobedience and satyagraha' both 'civil disobedience' and ' satyagraha' are deeply **interlinked** as a **theory of conflict resolution.**

Gandhi **emphasised** 'civil' in 'civil disobedience' to imply non-violence. **Non-violence**, as it is highlighted in the analysis, has a positive as well as a negative connotation.

In its *negative form*, it implies ' non-injury' to any living being. In its *positive form*, it means, 'the greatest love' and 'the greatest charity'. In Buddhist literature, it is highlighted as an attitude of creative coexistence.

The **Congress Party** organised the Civil Disobedience Movement in pursuance of the resolution on independence passed in the Lahore session of the Congress in **December 1929**. It was the result of British refusal to accept the Congress demand for Dominion Status. Factors such as the Lahore Conspiracy Case, the **tragic death of Jatin Das in jail in 1929**, the Meerut Conspiracy Case also forced the Congress to demand independence.

The civil disobedience movement got manifested in various forms such as the widespread defiance of law, **boycott** of **British** goods, withdrawal of support by the Army and the Police, and Non-co-operation with the government. **Gandhi highlighted** all these demands in his letter to the government in **1930** to break the salt law.

Gandhi **started his satyagraha** movement in **South Africa**. Subsequently, on his *return to India* to lead the non-co-operation movement against the British administration, he used it to remove the grievances of the oppressed workers and peasants of **Champaran, Kheda, and Bardoli.**

Gandhi has been taken to task for his emphasis on **self-suffering and satyagraha**. The Gandhian concept of satyagraha is **not merely an instrument** of conflict resolution or nonviolent resistance to **injustice**.

It is an **integrated concept**, covering the whole life process of a satyagrahi. **It includes:** truth, non-violence, chastity, non-stealing, swadeshi, fearlessness, breadlabour, removal of untouchability, and so on.

2. What is satyagraha? In what way does it differ from passive resistance?

Suggeseted Answer by INDIA EBOOK: Almost Same as Above **Q. No. 1**

3. What is the relevance of satyagraha and civil disobedience in the contemporary world?

Suggeseted Answer by INDIA EBOOK: **Mahatma Gandhi** is considered to be the leading theorist in the history of civil disobedience movement. The Gandhian concept of **civil disobedience and satyagraha** is the greatest contribution to mankind in our times.

Gandhi called his concept of civil disobedience as the **doctrine of 'Satyagraha' or 'Truth Force'.** For him, the adjective 'civil' in the phrase ' civil disobedience' referred to peaceful, courteous, and a 'civilised' resistance. To him, the concept of passive resistance is inadequate to grasp the full implications of the concept of 'satyagraha'. He said that one must not only resist passively the injustice and arbitrariness of the government, but also must do so without any feeling of animosity.

The **Gandhian concept** of civil disobedience and satyagraha has relevance in contemporary world. **Rabindranath Tagore** reflected the voice of the generation when he said, _Gandhi was a 'living truth', a symbol of humanism._

Gandhi used the civil disobedience method for the **first time during his march to Transvaal in South Africa in 1913** to protest against the discriminatory policies of the South African government. This was the first real mass movement of civil disobedience led by Gandhi. Gandhi was not interested in embarrassing the Smuts administration.

In **1918**, Gandhi used the civil disobedience movement in India during his campaign for the **textile workers** of Ahmedabad.

The **Salt Satyagraha of 1930**, the **civil disobedience movement** for independence in 1930, and his **fast unto death** for the development of social conditions of untouchables in 1939 are some of the examples of civil disobedience movements under the leadership of Gandhi in India.

The people of South Africa used the Gandhian method of civil disobedience to demand independence from the colonial administration. The civil disobedience movement against the apartheid policies of the South African Government in 1952, the **Johannesburg bus boycott in 1957**, and the 1960 march under the leadership of Chief Albert J Luthuli against the Sharpville massacre are some of the historic mass civil disobedience movements.

The Civil Disobedience movement by the **Buddhists in South Vietnam** against the American bombing was inspired by the doctrine of non-violence.

The other **historic examples** of civil disobedience movements were: the movement against German occupation in Denmark and Norway, Danilo Dolci's strike in Sicily in the 1950s, nuclear disarmament campaign in Western Europe, the non-violent demonstrations in Poland, the Vorkuta prison uprising in 1953 in the erstwhile Soviet Union, the Montgomery Civil rights march in 1955, and the anti-Vietnam war march towards the army base in Oakland in 1965.

The Civil Disobedience movement is gaining momentum day by day throughout the world.

4. What is Gandhi's contribution to the theory and practice of satyagraha?

Suggeseted Answer by INDIA EBOOK: **Gandhi** called his concept of civil disobedience as the **doctrine of 'Satyagraha' or 'Truth Force'.** For him, the adjective 'civil' in the phrase ' civil disobedience' referred to peaceful, courteous, and a 'civilised' resistance. To him, the concept of passive resistance is inadequate to grasp the full implications of the concept of 'satyagraha'. He said that one must not only resist passively the injustice and arbitrariness of the government, but also must do so without any feeling of animosity.

Gandhi **abandoned** the term 'passive resistance', and **chose the term 'satyagraha'.** The concept of satyagraha is devoid of any feelings of hatred and violent means. It is based on spiritual purity. Like Tolstoy, Gandhi was opposed to all forms of violence in his commitments to political actions.

Satyagraha, the **unique** system of **non-violent resistance** to the government's arbitrary methods and actions is, indeed, his **greatest gift to mankind.**

For Gandhi, **Ahimsa** (non-violence) and **Truth** were inseparable. He said that "Ahimsa is the means; Truth is the end." Gandhi used satyagraha as a lever for social movements.

Gandhi **strongly advocated** that it was the birth right of every individual to offer civil disobedience in the face of unjust laws.

The **Gandhian concept** of civil disobedience and satyagraha has relevance in contemporary world. **Rabindranath Tagore** reflected the voice of the generation when he said, *Gandhi was a 'living truth', a symbol of humanism.*

Gandhi used the civil disobedience method for the **first time during his march to Transvaal in South Africa in 1913** to protest against the discriminatory policies of the South African government. This was the first real mass movement of civil disobedience led by Gandhi. Gandhi was not interested in embarrassing the Smuts administration.

In **1918**, Gandhi used the civil disobedience movement in India during his campaign for the **textile workers** of Ahmedabad.

The **Salt Satyagraha of 1930**, the **civil disobedience movement** for independence in 1930, and his **fast unto death** for the development of social conditions of untouchables in 1939 are some of the examples of civil disobedience movements under the leadership of Gandhi in India.

The people of South Africa used the Gandhian method of civil disobedience to demand independence from the colonial administration. The civil disobedience movement against the apartheid policies of the South African Government in 1952, the **Johannesburg bus boycott in 1957**, and the 1960 march under the leadership of Chief Albert J Luthuli against the Sharpville massacre are some of the historic mass civil disobedience movements.

The Civil Disobedience movement by the **Buddhists in South Vietnam** against the American bombing was inspired by the doctrine of non-violence.

The other **historic examples** of civil disobedience movements were: the movement against German occupation in Denmark and Norway, Danilo Dolci's strike in Sicily in the 1950s, nuclear disarmament campaign in Western Europe, the non-violent demonstrations in Poland, the Vorkuta prison uprising in 1953 in the erstwhile Soviet Union, the Montgomery Civil rights march in 1955, and the anti-Vietnam war march towards the army base in Oakland in 1965.

The Civil Disobedience movement is gaining momentum day by day throughout the world.

5. What are the various dimensions of the Gandhian concept of satyagraha?

Hint: Write "INTRODUCTION" from Summary Concepts (under 150 words)

Then, Write the below Question Answer **June 2019: E-1** (under 350 words)

❑ PAST 8 ATTEMPTS IGNOU QUESTIONS

June 2019: E-1: Examine the Gandhian Concept of Civil Disobedience and Satyagrah.

Suggeseted Answer by INDIA EBOOK: **Mahatma Gandhi** is considered to be the leading theorist in the history of civil disobedience movement. The Gandhian concept of **civil disobedience and satyagraha** is the greatest contribution to mankind in our times.

Gandhi called his concept of civil disobedience as the **doctrine of 'Satyagraha' or 'Truth Force'.** For him, the adjective 'civil' in the phrase ' civil disobedience' referred to peaceful, courteous, and a 'civilised' resistance. To him, the concept of passive resistance is inadequate to grasp the full implications of the concept of 'satyagraha'. He said that one must not only resist passively the injustice and arbitrariness of the government, but also must do so without any feeling of animosity.

Gandhi **abandoned** the term 'passive resistance', and **chose the term 'satyagraha'**. The concept of satyagraha is devoid of any feelings of hatred and violent means. It is based on spiritual purity. Like Tolstoy, Gandhi was opposed to all forms of violence in his commitments to political actions.

Satyagraha, the **unique** system of **non-violent resistance** to the government's arbitrary methods and actions is, indeed, his **greatest gift to mankind.** For Gandhi, **Ahimsa** (non-violence) and **Truth** were inseparable. He said that "Ahimsa is the means; Truth is the end." Gandhi used satyagraha as a lever for social movements.

In order to understand the Gandhian concept of civil disobedience and satyagraha, it is desirable to know Gandhi's view on the subject in detail. Gandhi said, Satyagraha largely appears to the public as Civil

Disobedience or Civil Resistance. It is civil in the sense that it is **not criminal**.

Gandhi **strongly advocated** that it was the birth right of every individual to offer civil disobedience in the face of unjust laws.

In the concept of 'civil disobedience and satyagraha' both 'civil disobedience' and ' satyagraha' are deeply **interlinked** as a **theory of conflict resolution.**

Gandhi **emphasised** 'civil' in 'civil disobedience' to imply non-violence. **Non-violence**, as it is highlighted in the analysis, has a positive as well as a negative connotation.

The **Congress Party** organised the Civil Disobedience Movement in pursuance of the resolution on independence passed in the Lahore session of the Congress in **December 1929**. It was the result of British refusal to accept the Congress demand for Dominion Status. Factors such as the Lahore Conspiracy Case, the **tragic death of Jatin Das in jail in 1929**, the Meerut Conspiracy Case also forced the Congress to demand independence.

The civil disobedience movement got manifested in various forms such as the widespread defiance of law, **boycott** of **British** goods, withdrawal of support by the Army and the Police, and Non-co-operation with the government. **Gandhi highlighted** all these demands in his letter to the government in **1930** to break the salt law.

Gandhi **started his satyagraha** movement in **South Africa**. Subsequently, on his *return to India* to lead the non-co-operation movement against the British administration, he used it to remove the grievances of the oppressed workers and peasants of **Champaran, Kheda, and Bardoli.**

Gandhi has been taken to task for his emphasis on **self-suffering and satyagraha**. The Gandhian concept of satyagraha is **not merely an instrument** of conflict resolution or nonviolent resistance to **injustice**.

It is an **integrated concept**, covering the whole life process of a satyagrahi. **It includes:** truth, non-violence, chastity, non-stealing, swadeshi, fearlessness, breadlabour, removal of untouchability, and so on.

14. MPS-001: UNIT-14: Political Violence

- Introduction
- Meaning of Political Violence
- Violence and State – Political Violence & Political Integration; Process of Economic Development
- Causes of Political Violence – General Causes; Concept of national Self-Determination; Ideology; Religious & Ethnic Conflicts; Political Disputes between Elites; Relative Deprivation
- Forms of Political Violence – Violent Protest; Terrorism; Military Protest & Takeovers; Revolts & Rebellions; War
- Revolution – Meaning; Three(3) Phases; Theories
- Methods of Overcoming Political Violence
  - Methods of Reforms & Remedies
  - The Method of Force
  - The Policy of Carrot & Stick

IGNOU Book Exercise & Past 8 Attempts Questions - IMPORTANT

□ **IGNOU BOOK EXERCISE**

4. What are the **causes** of political violence?

Answer by India Ebook: **CAUSES OF POLITICAL VIOLENCE**

There are **many causes** that give birth to political violence. Men take recourse to violence as a last resort. It is rightly pointed out by **Aristotle** that men do not revolt because they catch cold.

People decide to use violent methods when they think that their **survival as a community is at stake** and unless they fight against it, they will have to have to suffer no end.

Normally, people exhaust legally available avenues to get their grievances redressed. But if the legal methods **fail** to deliver goods, people **take to violence.**

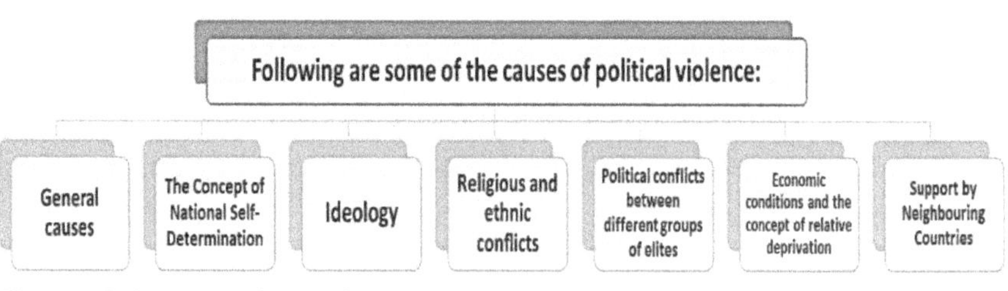

General Causes of Political Violence

Political violence has been a result of **bad government**. **Kautilya** in his **'Arthashastra'** said that *wrong policies of the government* and *immodest behaviour* of the **rulers** give **birth to revolts** of the people. Wrong and oppressive policies of the government create resentment in the minds of the people and the people rise violently to change the wrong policies.

Excessive taxation, hike in the prices of essential commodities, deliberate disregard of law and morality in the exercise of power, unjust treatment meted out to certain sections of society, deliberate neglect of certain regions of the state, political incompetence and misgovernment and excessive and tactless use of force to put down peaceful agitation are the general causes of violence. Kautilya held that impoverishment, greed and disaffection are the causes of revolt.

The Concept of National Self-Determination

During the last two centuries, a large number of countries of Third World came under foreign control. They became colonies of Western countries. People in the Third world countries wanted to free themselves from foreign domination. Hence, they waged violent struggles against foreign rule. In modern times, the American settlers were the first to take to arms to free their country from British rule.

We have numerous examples of such struggles in Afro-Asian countries such as Vietnam, Algeria and Indonesia. Due to the pacifist ideas of **Mahatma Gandhi**, the Indian liberation movement remained largely **non-violent**, though there were certain armed revolutionaries like **Sawarkar Bagha Jatin**, **Bhagat Singh** and **Subhash Chandra Bose** in India also.

The supporters of national self-determination movement called it a movement for national liberation while the opponents of these movements called them secessionist movements. In India, we are facing these type of movements in Jammu and Kashmir, Nagaland, Manipur and Assam. Most of the Third World countries are facing this problem.

The **Irish Republican Army** and the **LTTE in Srilanka** are the most dreaded separatist groups in the world. These movements are marked by excessive use of violence from both the sides. Thus, nationalism caused the emergence of national liberation movements as well as the movements for national self-determination.

Ideology

In modern times, **ideology has played an important role** in the spread of political violence. Ideology mobilises people and gives them a certain cause to wage struggle against the state. Ideology explains the present conditions of society and asks the people to change it to bring about a better system of governance. Most of the movements in modern times are **ideological in character**. **Fascism and socialism** were two such **ideologies.**

Fascist ideas became popular in Europe between the **two World Wars**. Fascists glorified force and violence and advocated the unity of interests of individuals with that of the nation state. **Fascism in Italy** and **Nazism in Germany** used the extreme form of violence to capture political power. The ideology of revolutionary socialism moved a large number of people who were involved in violent revolutionary activities. The socialists stand for the abolition of the capitalist system, which is based on state violence.

The **socialists** want to establish a **classless** and **stateless** society which would **end exploitation** of man by man. We have examples of successful revolutions like the **Russian revolution**, The **Chinese revolution** and The **Cuban revolution**. In **India**, the **Naxalites** are involved in revolutionary political activities.

Religious and Ethnic Conflicts

Most of the countries of the world are inhabited by the people who adhere to *different religious faiths* and belong to **different ethnic**

communities. Therefore, there are **religious and ethnic minorities** in most of the countries.

Religious and ethnic minorities resist this attempt because they fear that due to this political integration they may lose their separate identity. The moment force is applied to advance this policy these communities take recourse to resistance and violence.

Many of the West European countries witnessed religious conflicts during the 17th and 18th centuries. The conflict was between the Catholics and the Protestants. Now, modern European states claim that they are secular and they have achieved separation between the church and the state.

Inter-religious conflicts take place between two religious communities, between Christians and Muslims, Jews and Muslims or Hindus and Muslims. There is intra-religious conflict within a particular religious community when a particular religious sect wants to purge the religion of corrupt practices. The fundamentalist groups, who want to purify their religion, take to an extreme form of violence.

Culturally and ethnically, modern societies **are not homogenous**. Cultural and ethnic minorities want to preserve their separate identity. Hence, they want to secure and protect their rights. These minorities are formed on the basis of race, language and culture.

Nagaland in India, Northern Ireland in Great Britain, the Chechens in Russia, Tibetans in China and Kurds in Iraq and Iran are **examples** of this.

Political Disputes between Different Groups of the Elites

Governing elite in each state consists of groups, factions, and these groups and factions are involved in power politics. These groups and factions use violent methods to secure support of the people by organising street demonstrations, communal riots and sabotage.

A group, well established in the government uses coercive powers of state institutions to curb this violence. Political disputes among the elite may result in splits and divisions in the ruling group.

The dissident group many incite violence against the ruling group or take help of a faction in the army to capture political power. Sometimes, the disgruntled leaders may support the secessionist movements. Many a times, the military take over is the result of such disputes.

The Afghan history after 1972, military take overs in Pakistan and Bangladesh are examples of this type of politics. These military takeovers are often very violent and cause a large-scale bloodshed.

Economic Conditions and the Concept of Relative Deprivation

Economic conditions give birth to different types of political violence because they generate resentment in the minds of the people. It is the wrong policies of the government that favour certain sections of the society and push a large section of the people below poverty line.

Due to the wrong policies of the government, there is growing inflation, declining living standards of the people, price rise, unemployment and non-availability of essential commodities in the market. These factors force people to take to streets and participate in violent demonstrations against the government.

Support by Neighbouring Countries

Political violence, especially sustained political violence in a state always gets support from the neighbouring countries, which are hostile. The foreign country gives support in the form of arms, money, training and shelter.

For example, political violence in **Jammu and Kashmir** is supported by Pakistan. America gave support to rebels in Cuba and Nicaragua and Libya and Iraq are accused of supporting the Islamic terrorist network.

9. Write a note on the **theories of revolution.**

Answer by India Ebook: Revolution is essentially a modern phenomenon because it wants to bring about a total transformation of society. Revolutions are marked by widespread violence, social unrest and ideological commitment. The new revolutionary ideology is radical, rational, democratic and universal.

Modern revolutions are not confined to replacing a bad ruler with a good one but they have a modernist agenda of restructuring the entire socio-political order by the legitimate representatives of the community.

Meaning of Revolution

As we have seen, revolutions are aimed at changing the basic structure of society. They want to bring about a rapid transformation of the society's state and class structures. This is accompanied and carried through by the class based revolts from below.

Modern revolutions differ from the earlier revolts in the sense that the latter did not think of basic changes in society and state and they were more interested in change in the government. Modern revolution has its goals clearly defined and its leaders use violence to consummate it. Its leaders are backed by a well-defined theory which seeks to legitimise revolutionary violence.

Three Phases of Revolution

We can say that there are three distinct phases of revolution. The first phase of revolution is the classical phase. The second phase of revolution is the socialist phase and the third phase of revolution is revolution in the Third World countries.

The **classical phase** of revolution began in England during the British Civil War of the 17th century that destroyed royal absolutism in England. It was followed by the French Revolution of 1789, which witnessed unprecedented violence and bloodshed. It destroyed feudalism in France and paved the way for the emergence of the modern capitalist society. The American Revolution ended foreign domination and established a modern constitutional democracy in USA. All these three revolutions transformed state organisations, class structures and dominant ideologies.

The classical revolutions were followed by the **socialist revolutions** of the 20th century. It began with the October Revolution of 1917 in Russia. It was succeeded by the Chinese Revolution in 1949 and the Cuban Revolution in 1961. Ideologically, the leaders of these revolutions were more radical in the sense that they wanted to have a total transformation of social, economic and political structures. Though all socialist revolutionaries believed in Marxist philosophy and Leninist politics of international proletarian revolution, they followed different methods to bring about the revolution.

In the **third phase**, revolutions were witnessed in the third world countries. The Egyptian revolt of 1953 paved the way for the emergence of new politics in Arab countries. The Islamic revolution of Iran in 1979 was the last of the great revolutions, which tried to reorder Iranian society on the principles of radical Islam.

Theories of Revolution

There are three distinct theories of revolution.

The **first theory** of revolution is expounded by **Ted Robert Gurr** in his book 'Why Men Rebel!' He says that revolution is a form of political violence and it challenges the monopoly of force possessed by the state. He is of the view that turmoil, conspiracy and internal war are the three features of revolution. The main cause of disaffection and rebellion is relative deprivation of the people. The more intense the deprivation, the greater is the degree of violence. He thinks that at first, there is discontent of the people, then there is politicisation of discontent and finally, its actualisation in violent action against the state. He holds that the discontented elite plays a major role in revolution.

C. Johnson tried to understand revolution as a systemic imbalance. He is of the opinion that revolution takes place due to the development of social imbalances and systemic disequilibrium. These imbalances are caused because of the changes in the values of people. He thinks that the first cause of revolution is power deflation. Second cause is the inability of the legitimate leaders to effect' synchronisation' to overcome power deflation.

The **third** theory of revolution is the **Marxist theory**, which believes in class warfare. According to Marx, our known history is a history of class struggle between haves and have nots and the contradiction between them come in the open in the capitalist state of development.

METHODS OF OVERCOMING POLITICAL VIOLENCE

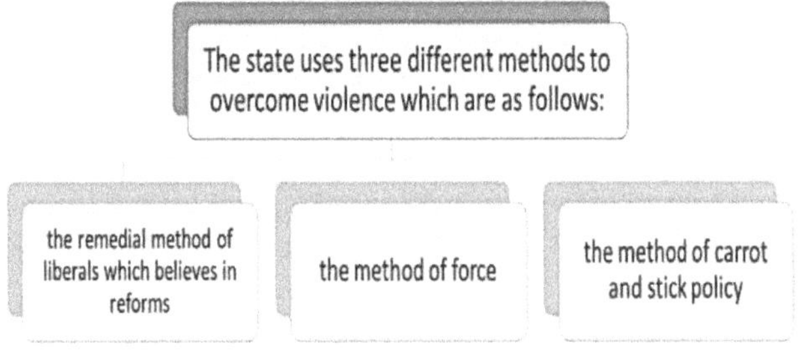

❏ PAST 8 ATTEMPTS IGNOU QUESTIONS

June 2019: E-1: Define Political Violence and Discuss its various forms.

Answer by India Ebook: **Political violence** is a collective violent action of a group of people against the government to highlight its discontent. It may be a **protest against** a particular **policy of the government**, it may be used to remove a particular government from power, or it may be taken recourse to for the change of political system.

Aggression and violence have been a part of human history since long because men take to violence and aggression to secure things that they did not possess or to preserve things that they possessed. Normally, political violence is directed against the state, its property and men who manage its institutions. Political violence may begin with rioting or mass demonstrations. But it is always possible that it assumes different forms.

Aristotle was the first political scientist who discussed the nature and causes of political disorder. He pointed out that change in the balance of social forces in a particular state was responsible for political disorder.

The Indian political thinker **Kautilya (Chanakya)** was of the opinion that change in the attitude of one's own people is **revolt.** It results from a **wrong policy** of the government and **immodest behaviour** of the **king.**

Thus, since **ancient times**, political violence had caused disorder in the state and in modern times, the problem of political violence has become more marked and complex.

FORMS OF POLITICAL VIOLENCE

There exist different forms of political violence, which people use to show their resentment and dissatisfaction against the government. It can assume a form of a violent demonstration or it can be an epoch making revolution like the French revolution of 1789.

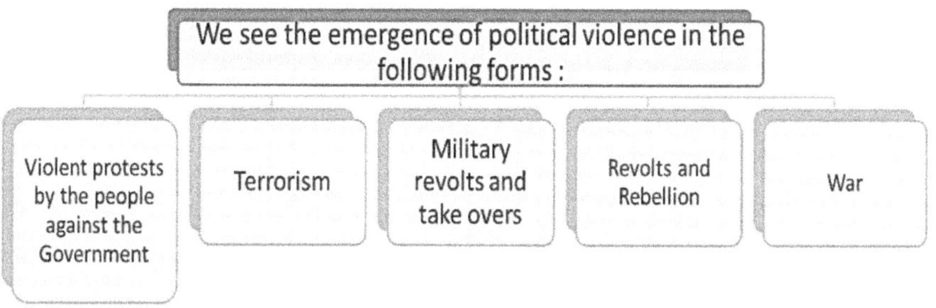

Violent Protest by the People against the Government

Normally, people take recourse to violence when all the constitutional means available to them fail. The violent protests of the people assume different forms. The violent protests of unorganised mobs cause a large scale damage because they attack the symbols of government authority such as government offices, railways and buses. They try to disrupt normal functioning of the government. They declare strikes, 'bandhs', and hartals.

Terrorism

In modern times, terrorism has become one of the important forms of political violence as a large number of young people join terrorist groups to bring about change in the government. The weapon of terrorism is used by terrorists because they know that they cannot launch an open war against the state as the state has a superior force at its command. Their power in society is also based on the gun.

They get involved in activities of sabotage, murder, killing a large number of people in sudden gun fire, hijacking of an aircraft or a bus, holding people for ransom, kidnapping, political assassinations, extortions, setting fire to places of worship and markets, inciting caste and communal riots etc.

Military Revolts and Take Overs

In modern times, the military or the armed forces of the country are playing an important role in the politics of the third world countries because they are the only well organised force available in societies which have not undergone the process of state and nation building.

Involvement of military in political violence assumes two forms 1) the mutiny of soldiers and 2) military take over or 'coup detat'.

All over the world disgruntled elements in the armed forces rebel against the government. This revolt is called mutiny. Due to some economic or political reasons, the soldiers take to arms and get involved in violent activities.

For example, in **1857 the Indian soldiers** of the army of British East India Company revolted against the British rule and killed a large number of their British officers.

The **second form** of political violence is the military take over by engineering a 'coup detat'. Military takeover is a sharp armed insurrection by a group of army officers to capture political power by establishing control over key installations of the state. It is a well organised operation in which masses are bypassed. If coup leaders are confident of controlling the situation, they may not take recourse to violence.

For example, The military coup in Indonesia in 1965-66 was extremely violent. All military takeovers in Afghanistan after 1973 were violent.

Revolts and Rebellions

We have seen that terrorist violence or even military revolts do not need the support of the masses. It is essentially an action carried out by a determined group of people. But revolts and rebellions take place because of popular disaffection.

Revolts represent the anger of certain sections of society and they are aimed at changing the policy of the government or change in the government. The revolts may take place in different parts of the country and the demands of the rebels may be very specific.

If the revolts are accompanied by a high degree of organisation and with the tacit approval of wide sections of the population, one can say that they have assumed a serious form. It includes large scale terrorism and civil war. The **revolt may develop into a rebellion.**

The rebels normally use the tactics of **guerilla warfare** because they lack the military strength to counter state forces. To circumvent the armed superiority of the state, the guerillas try to win the support of the people through the ideological exhortations or through the promises of redistributive policy.

They promise land to the landless, regional autonomy for ethnic minorities and political equality through the end of foreign domination. The revolutionary guerilla warfare succeeded in countries like China, Vietnam and Cuba but it failed in Greece, Philippines and Iran.

War

War is the culmination of political violence in the sense that war brings forth two contending forces face to face with each other and settles the issue on the basis of balance of armed forces. War is as old as human history and violence and bloodshed are at the heart of it. There are two types of wars :

1) war with the external enemy of the country and

2) internal war, which takes place between the state forces and the rebels (civil war).

The external war causes widespread damage and destruction because both the parties use massive armies, modern weapons of mass destruction and air force. The **First World War** accounted for a million deaths and the Second World War was the most destructive of all wars. Atomic weapons were used by the USA to settle the issue.

Internal war is fought between the forces of a central government and the secessionist forces. It could be a revolt by a certain sections of the people or a rebellion by the broad mass of people. In the 1860s, the USA witnessed a civil war between the northern and the southern states on the issue of the abolition of slavery. Internal war is equally destructive and it may cause widespread destruction and massacres. We have examples of violent internal wars in Lebanon, Yugoslavia, Nigeria and India.

Thus, political violence assumes different forms in modern times. Revolution is also a particular form of political violence.

15. MPS-001: UNIT-15: Classical Liberalism

- Introduction
- What is Liberalism?
- Characteristics of Liberalism
- Rise of Liberalism
- Ideology of Classical Liberalism – Views on Man, Society, Economy and State
- Critical Evaluation
- Exercise & Past 8 Attempts Questions

IGNOU Book Exercise & Past 8 Attempts Questions - IMPORTANT

❑ **IGNOU BOOK EXERCISE**

1. Explain the concept and characteristics of liberalism.

Answer by India Ebook: Liberalism is the **dominant ideology** of the present-day Western world. The history of England, Western Europe and America for the last 300 years is closely associated with the evolution and development of liberal thought.

Liberalism was the **product of the climate** of opinion that emerged at the time of the Renaissance and Reformation in Europe. As **an ideology** and a way of life, 'it **reflected** the economic, social and political aspirations of the rising middle class which later on became the capitalist class'.

Liberalism is the dominant ideology of the present-day western world. It was the: product of the climate of opinion that merged in the context of renaissance, reformation and industrial revolution in England and Europe.

As **AL blaster** writes, 'liberalism should be seen not as a fixed at-id absolute term, as a collection of unchanging moral and political values belt as a specific historical movement of ideas in the modern era that began with Renaissance and Reformation. It has undergone many changes and requires a historical rather than a static type of analysis.'

Similarly, **Laski** writes, 'it (Liberalism) is not easy to describe, much less to define, for it is hardly less a habit of mind than a body of doctrine'.

Liberalism is not merely a political concept, but also a socio-economic, cultural and ethical concept. It can be understood through certain characteristics evolved during its long history. **John Hallowell** has pinpointed the following characteristics of classical liberalism:

i. a belief in the absolute value of human personality and spiritual equality of the individual;

ii. a belief in the autonomy of the individual will;

iii. a belief in the essential rationality and goodness of man;

iv. a belief in certain inalienable rights of the individual, paltitularly, the rights of life, liberty and property;

v. that state comes into existence by mutual consent for the purpose of protection of rights;

vi. that the relationship between the state and the individual is a contractual one;

vii. that social control can best be secured by law rather than command;

viii. Individual freedom in all spheres of life - political, economic, social, intellectual and religious;

ix. the government that governs the least is the best;

x. a belief that truth is accessible to man's natural reason.

16. MPS-001: UNIT-16: Welfare State

- Introduction
- Evolution of Positive Liberalism – Welfare State is Positive; Democratic; Mixed Economy; Neutral Agency
- Justification of the Welfare State
- State & the Market; Individualist; Enhances Individual Liberty; Equality; Rights; Citizenship; Justice
- Welfare State – Contemporary Debate
- Crisis in the Welfare State – Assessment
- Exercise & Past 8 Attempts Questions

IGNOU Book Exercise & Past 8 Attempts Questions - IMPORTANT

❑ IGNOU BOOK EXERCISE

1. Trace the evolution of positive liberalism.

Answer by India Ebook: Negative liberalism believed that the distribution of wealth into wage, profit and rent was **not unjustified**. However, the latter half of the **19th century** saw the rapid concentration of capital in a few hands, monopolistic control of trade, and emergence of big industrial houses which created many social, economic and political contradictions.

In fact, the liberal slogan of liberty began to change into the **privilege of the few**. In **England**, the report or the **Royal Commission** appointed to investigate the coal mining industry shocked everyone about the brutality that existed in the mines, the employment of women and children, barbarously long hours of work, the absence of safety devices and the prevalence of revolting conditions, both physical and moral.

Classical liberalism became a **target of attack from all sides**. The humanists criticized it due to its practical consequences such as poverty, inhuman conditions, unbearable exploitation, illiteracy and misery for the majority of the population.

A thoroughgoing revision of **liberal theory** required a re-examination of the nature and functions of the state, the nature of liberty and the relationship between Liberty and authority. Such a re-examination also opened the question of the relationship between individual human nature and its relations with society because the old notions such as self-interest, pleasure and utility proved less convincing. **This revision is known as**

'Positive Liberalism' and was carried out by J.S. Mill, T.H. Green, D.G. Ritchie in the 19th century and Hobson, Hobhouse, Lindsay, G.D.H. Cole, Barker, Laski, Keynes, MacIver and Galbraith in the 20th century.

In short, **positive liberalism** as it evolved during the later half of the 19th and the first half of the 20th centuries could be distinguished from classical negative liberalism in many ways.

Firstly, although it continued to retain faith in the autonomy, rights and liberty of the individual, now it believed that man is a part of the social whole and the liberties could be secured only so long as they could be reconciled with the social good. Society was considered a potential harmonious and ordered structure in which all social classes work for the common good.

Secondly, liberty, like justice and equality, is not an empty social ideal, but derives its specific content from a particular social and historical milieu in which it has to be understood. Liberty in the society implied adjustment of mutual claims that are made possible through a system or rights which are both restraints and liberties.

Thirdly, positive liberalism believed in regulated capitalist economy, in the overall interest of society. The state could check the individual capitalist, through economic and social reforms, the conditions of the working class could be improved; poverty, illiteracy, unemployment and exploitation could be checked. The gap between the rich and the poor could be bridged through the positive action of the state.

Fourthly, at the political level, positive liberalism depended upon the proposition that the sense of public good or general welfare is an effective motive of politics. The state is an instrument for the development of human personality through welfare measures. The state has a positive character and is capable of performing socially useful functions.

The institutional arrangements for achieving the good of the individual and the society are democracy, representative government, constitutionalism, parliamentary methods, universal franchise, party organization. The liberal government is one which protects the rights of the individual as well as of the community. The state is to coordinate different interests and classes in society. It does not belong to a particular class, but to the society as a whole.

2. Write an essay on the liberal democratic welfare state.

Answer by India Ebook: The **welfare state** attempted to reconcile the interests of the individual with that of the society in order the essentials of the capitalist system were preserved while at the same time removing its ill-effects.

The object of the state is not only to maintain law, order and justice, but it is also a part of the social process, its function in the society is to serve the common interests and perform services for the welfare of all members of the society. The main principles of the welfare state are relatively simple.

Firstly, the recognition that every member of the community, solely because he is a human being, is entitled to a minimum standard of living.

Secondly, the welfare state is committed to a policy of economic stability and progress, seeking to eliminate the cycles of violent booms and busts in the economy by public policies, whenever private enterprise is unable to prevent by itself the threat of economic in stability or decline.

Thirdly, the welfare state is committed to full employment as one of the top priorities of public policy. The economic depression of the **1930s** showed not only the economic ravages of unemployment, but also the human degradation inflicted upon those who though able and anxious to work, could not find jobs for reasons over which they had no control.

Through the instrument of welfare, positive liberalism used the power of the state to modify the play of market forces in at least three directions:
i) by guaranteeing individuals and families a minimum income irrespective of the market value of their work or property,
ii) by narrowing the content of insecurity by enabling individuals and families to meet certain social contingencies such as sickness, old age and unemployment, and
iii) by ensuring that all citizens without distinction of status or class are offered the best available agreed range of social services.

The distinguishing characteristic of the welfare state is the assumption by the community, acting through the state, of the responsibility of providing the means whereby all its members can reach minimum standard of health, economy and civilized living and can share, according to their capacity, in its social and cultural heritage. The welfare state has the following unique features.

Welfare State is a Positive State

The underlying assumption behind the welfare state is that the state is not a necessary evil, but a desirable institution capable of promoting positive good. Whereas the *laissez faire* liberalism contended that the government an advance the common interest by leaving the individual alone and through the free and unrestricted play of natural forces, the exponents of welfare state argued that 'the state could best promote the general welfare by a positive exercise of its powers'.

Welfare State is a Democratic

The **neo-liberals** categorically asserted that the **welfare state** is a democratic state, possessing a certain formal institutional mechanism which is considered essential in liberal democratic society. Any state which may be a welfare state, but is not democratic from the institutional point of view, cannot be regarded a liberal state.

Welfare State believes in a Mixed Economy

A welfare state operates within the framework of the market economy i.e. the capitalist mode of production. However, unlike the **laissez faire** capitalist economy, the welfare state believes that unrestricted operation of the market has proved dangerous for the individual as well as for the economy.

Welfare State is a Permanent Institution of Society and a Neutral Agency

The welfare state, positive liberalism maintains, is an eternal and permanent institution of society. The state is also a neutral instrument of power which can be used for any purpose.

17. MPS-001: UNIT-17: Libertarianism

➤ Exercise & Past 8 Attempts Questions

WHAT IS LIBERTARIANISM (Explain in your own Words – Q.1 of Book) – [Dec 2019]

Ansswer by India Ebook: The **libertarian philosophy** has been **propounded** by a number of scholars, prominent among them are FA Hayek, Karl Popper, Talmon, Milton Friedman, I. Berlin, M. Rothbard, Robert Nozick, Ayn Rand. Taking Liberty as the ultimate value, it asserts that in order to protect liberty, a society must have strong private property rights, a free market and minimal government. **Some writers** have termed **libertarianism as freedom**.

The best way to understand the various terms is to know what libertarians believe in. In a few words, libertarianism believes that individual freedom is the fundamental value that must underlie all social relations, economic exchanges and the political system. Essentially libertarians preach freedom in all fields including the right to do what one wants with one's own body insofar as one does not infringe on the property and equal freedom of others.

They believe that **voluntary cooperation** between individuals in a **free market** is always preferable to **coercion** exerted by the **State**. They believe that the role of the State is not to pursue goals in the name of **community**. The **State** is not there to **redistribute wealth**, promote culture, **support the agriculture sector** or help small firms, but should limit itself to the protection of individual rights and let citizens pursue their own goals in a peaceful way.

Libertarianism is **opposed to collectivist ideologies** of all types, be it of the left or of the right which stress the primacy of the group, nation, social class, sexual or ethnic group, religious or language community etc. They oppose all whose purpose is to regiment it individuals in the pursuit of collective goals.

Thus, libertarianism rejects the main political developments of the **20**[th] **century**; that is, the **sustained growth** in the size of the state and the range of its interventions in the private lives of the citizens. The libertarian movement hardly existed in the **1960s** but really took off in the **Unites States** in the **early 1970s**. After a century of eclipse, **classical**

liberalism in its libertarian off spring is becoming an influential philosophical doctrine and movement in the **21st century**.

Like all philosophical movements, libertarianism is varied, containing several schools and sub-groups and one will find no unanimity about its theoretical justifications, its goals or the strategy that should be adopted to reach them. Mainly, there are two types of libertarianism and each has its own answers to the queries.

One group, the **anarchists** or also known as 'anarcho-capitalists' advocate the complete disappearance of the State and Privatisation of even the basic functions mentioned above. This goal may appear extreme or ridiculous at first sight, but it is based on a theoretically plausible argument.

The **other** branch is known as 'miniarchists' who maintain that government may appropriately engage in police protection, enforcement of contracts and national defence, foreign relations, justice, the protection of private property and individual rights. All remaining functions should be privatised.

The **question arises**: Why the **libertarians endorse** these views so sharply at **variance** with most **political theory**?

Firstly, libertarians hold an extremely strong doctrine of individual rights, particularly the right of individuals to acquire and hold property.

Secondly, libertarians believe that the operation of an unrestricted system of laissez faire capitalism is the most desirable social system.

Solved IGNOU Book Exercise & Solved Past 8 Attempts Questions

❏ **PAST 8 ATTEMPTS IGNOU QUESTIONS**

Dec 2019: E-1: What is Libertarianism? Explain.

Answer by India Ebook: Exact same as of Above.

18. MPS-001: UNIT-18: Marxism-I
Marx, Lenin, Mao

- ➢ Introduction
- ➢ Karl Marx (1818 – 1833) : Alienation; Historical Materialism; Class War; Surplus Value
- ➢ V. I. Lenin (1870 – 1924) : Party as Vanguard of the Proletariat; Democratic Centralism; Imperialism; Weakest Link of the Chain; Spontaneity Element gives way to Selectivity of Time & Place
- ➢ Mao Tse-Tung (now Mao Zedong) (1893 – 1976)
  - o Peasant Revolution
  - o Contradictions
  - o On Practice
  - o United Front and New Democracy
- ➢ Exercise & Past 8 Attempts Questions

VVI: MUST DO FULL

UNIT-18

<table><tr><td>**KARL MARX (1818 – 1883)**</td><td>[Q.1 of Book]</td></tr></table>

Born at Trier in **Germany** in **1818** (May 5) **Marx** studied law at the University of Bonn and later at the University of Berlin where lie got attracted to the young **Hegelian movement** which was highly critical not only of the **Prussian Government**, but also of Christianity. Because of his association with this **anti-government movement**, his career options in university or government were virtually closed.

The **central concern** of this work is **alienation**. It was also during his stay at **Paris** that he met **Friedrich Engels** who became his life long friend and benefactor. However, because of his revolutionary ideas Marx was expelled from France as well in **1844** and (along with Engels) **he moved to Belgium**.

During his stay in **Belgium**, spanning over three years, Marx got involved in a serious study of history which led him to propound his famous theory of historical materialism or materialistic interpretation of history. This theory is contained in the **first joint work** of **Marx** and **Engels** titled, The German Ideology.

Around this time, he **joined** the **Communist League**, which was an organisation of emigrant German Workers. When the League held its conference at London in **1847**, Marx & Engels were assigned the task of writing a **Communist Manifesto**. It was the publication of this work in 1848 which led to a wave of workers revolutions in Europe, more particularly in France.

Marx's analysis of these revolutions is contained in two works: i) The **Class Struggle in France** ii) The **18th Brumaire of Louis Bonaparte**. In 1848, Marx returned to France & from there to Germany where he again started the publication of his earlier newspaper **Rheinische Zeitung**. Like its earlier stance, the paper was highly critical of the Prussian Govt & it was again closed down by the authorities. in 1949 (May) Marx moved to England & stayed at London till his death in 1883.

Marx's 34 years stay in England is marked by two changes in him. **Firstly**, he moved gradually but decisively from Philosophy to Economics. Unlike alienation which is the central theme of EPM, Marx now got engrossed in the analysis of the phenomenon of exploitation. He devoted his attention to serious questions like wage labour, capitalism & surplus value.

Secondly, he was as much involved in writing serious treaties as in leading the workers' movement in Europe. He was not merely an arm-chair theoretician critical of capitalism, and its exploitative nature but also a revolutionary & an ideology of communism. His most incisive work in this direction was a massive manuscript titled "**Grundrisse**" (Outline) which he wrote around **1857** but which came to light only in **1939**.

His thesis about labour theory of value, surplus value & laws of capital accumulation are contained in his three volume magnum opus Capital whose first volume came out in 1867 and the remaining **two volumes** were published by **Engels** after Marx's death.

Marx's stay in London was also devoted to organising the **British** and French workers. In 1864 he (along with others) set up the first major organisation of workers of Europe which was named "International Working Men's Association (popularly known as **Communist International**).

It remained active up to 1876 & its brightest hour was in 1871 when it succeeded in setting up the **Paris Commune.** The workers of Paris captured the city & ruled it for nearly two months. **Marx's Civil War in France** written in 1871 is an elaboration of the aims anti-working of the Paris Commune. After 1870, Marx was mostly reacting to various political developments which were taking place in Europe. This criticism is contained in his Critique of the Gotha Programme (1875).

Alienation

Marx in his early years was attracted to **Hegelian idealism**, but under the influence of Feuerbach lie embraced communism of the humanist variety which he articulated in his EPM. He criticized capitalism because it leads to the alienation of labour. It is only in communism that human beings will be redeemed from this phenomenon.

Alienation is a very complex concept. Sometimes it is equated with such concepts as estrangement, objectification and reification. To put it in simple words, it implies de-humanization or the loss of self. The worker in a capitalist order works in a mechanical manner & does not derive any pleasure from his work. His labour becomes a commodity which he must sell in order to survive.

Thus, lie gets alienated from his work. He is also alienated from the product of his labour, from his fellow workers and from the natural world. Marx argued that in a capitalist society, the worker is alienated from the product of his labour because it does not belong to him but belongs to somebody else (the capitalist). The competitive nature of capitalism also alienates the worker from his fellow workers.

In essence, the worker is alienated from his creative potentialities that are characteristic of his species being. Marx advocated that it is only in a communist society that man will return to his real self as a free creative agent & the work will no more remain a monotonous activity.

Private property is the product and the consequence of alienated labour and, therefore, its abolition will lead to redemption of man his alienated state.

Historical Materialism [Q.2 of Book]

In the history of ideas there are **three** main explanations of how the **human societies** have developed over the ages - the spiritualist interpretation, the idealist interpretation and the materialist interpretation. According to the **first**, all developments in human history are due to divine dispensation or God's will. According to the **second**, it is the ideas that constitute the motor of human history. According to the third, which Marx expounded, all developments in human history are due to changes in the material conditions of life.

In the idealist interpretation it is the mind which is primary and matter secondary; while according to **Marx's materialist** interpretation, it is matter which is primary and the mind secondary. The doctrine of historical materialism constitutes the core of Marxian writings.

It is the main theme of **Marx's German Ideology**. It seeks to explain all historical events in terms of changes occurring in the mode of production. The changes from primitive communism to slavery, from slavery to feudalism, from feudalism to capitalism to socialism & communism are all explained in terms of changes in the material conditions of society & in the lives of individuals.

The mode of production consists of the forces or **means of production** (land, labour, capital, machine tools and factories, etc.) and relations of productions: slave-master, serf-baron, proletariat-capitalist. The economic structure of each society which is constituted by relations of production is the real foundation of that society.

Marx's theory of historical materialism is also dialectical. Marx borrowed the dialectical method from Hegel who had described all the historical changes in terms of thesis, anti-thesis & synthesis in the domain of ideas. An idea (thesis), according to Hegal, gives rise to a counter-idea (anti-thesis) and finally their contradiction is resolved in a synthesis.

Class War

The mode of production or the way social production is organised in a society and the way instruments of production are used for such production determines social, political, legal and ideological character of society. At a certain stage, the forces of production out-grow (develop) beyond the relations of production and get out of tune with the existing relations of production which fetter (hinder) the former's growth.

This contradiction (opposition) between the **forces of production & relations of production** leads to a **class war**, i.e., a war between the class which owns the means of production & the class which owns only labour power. Class War, according to Marx, has been the most prominent & recurring feature of all human societies.

When this class war reaches a **water mark & contradictions** become intense, it is resolved through a social revolution which ensures newer & higher relations of production corresponding to the forces or means of production. But, in due course, the forces of production again outgrow the relations of production again necessitating a social revolution. This process goes on.

A marked feature of a class-based society is that antagonism or contradiction arises due to divergent economic interests. In order to defend its class interest, the class owning the means of production establishes its class rule. "**No antagonism, no progress**" asserted **Marx**.

You can see from the above argument that **Marx's contention** is that the state in a capitalist society is a vehicle of class rule. It follows from this argument that if classes are abolished and a class-less society comes about, then the state will become redundant and gradually it will wither away.

Surplus Value [Dec 2019]

Another important theory that **Marx** enunciated is the theory of **surplus value**. It is with the help of this concept that Marx explained the whole phenomenon of exploitation in the capitalist society. To put it in simple terms, surplus value is what is normally called profit.

Marx's argument is that the worker produces social objects which are sold by the capitalist for more than what the worker receives as "**wages**". Thus, the worker is not paid for the whole of **his labour** (or labour power) that he spends in producing the social commodities. Some part of his labour is appropriated (or stolen) by the capitalist.

The theory of *surplus value is rooted* in the **labour theory of value** i.e., that value of a commodity depends on the amount of labour spent in producing it. In other words, surplus value arises because some part of the worker's labour is not paid to him.

As pointed out above, this gives *rise to a sharp contradiction* between the **bourgeoisie** and the **proletariat** which is resolved finally in a **proletarian revolution**. This revolution will bring about the demise of **capitalism**. The state power will be captured by the proletariat. After the capture of state power by the working class, Marx visualized a brief period of dictatorship of the proletariat.

It is during this **dictatorship** that the society would usher in socialism (where each will work according to capacity and get according to work) and finally, communism(where each will work according to capacity and get according to need). Thus, communism is viewed by **Marx** as a class less society of associated producers.

Communism for **Marx** was a society which **revolutionary dictatorship** of the proletariat would bring about after capitalism is overthrown. It will also undertake positive abolition of private property & the abolition of private ownership. In a Communist society, there will neither be exploitation nor alienation.

V. I. LENIN (1870-1924)

- Party as Vanguard of the Proletariat
- Democratic Centralism
- Imperialism
- Weakest Link of the Chain
- Spontaneity Element gives way to Selectivity of Time & Place

V. I. LENIN (1870 – 1924)

Born at **Simbirsk** in 1870 (April 22) **Lenin** had normal schooling. However, when he was taking his final school examination at the age of **16 his elder brother (Alexander)** was charged of **conspiring to kill the Tsar** (King in Russia was known as Tsar) and was sentenced to death by the Tsarist regime.

Despite all the trauma that this event brought to **Lenin**, he secured the highest possible marks in the school examination. After school education, he joined the Kazan University. It was during his stay at the University that Lenin began taking part in the various student agitations which ultimately led to his expulsion from the University.

Thereafter, he involved himself fully in revolutionary activities and soon became the leader of the Marxist group at **St. Petersburg**. He was arrested in 1895 by the Tsarist regime and exiled to Siberia. It was here that he wrote his first major work **"Development of Capitalism in Russia"** (1899).

In this work, he described how capitalism was growing in **Russia** during its initial phase. In **1900** he migrated to **Geneva** and joined **Plakhanov's revolutionary group**. He also started editing a paper named **Iskara** in which lie launched an anti-Tsarist campaign. In **1902**, he wrote his second important work - What is to be done which deals with party organisation.

In **1916** when the **first world war** had reached a very grim stage, Lenin produced his most incisive work Imperialism, the Highest Stage of

Capitalism wherein he analysed the phenomenon of imperialism. In October **1917**, he assumed power in **Russia.**

Party as Vanguard of the Proletariat [Q.3 of Book]

There are several seminal contributions of **Lenin to Marxist** theory and practice. In his **Development of Capitalism** in **Russia,** he tried to offer an interpretation of Tsarist **Russia in Marxist terms.** He argued that there was a large **wage-labour** class in **Russia.** However, he expressed the view that this wage labour class was not fully conscious of its exploitation.

He further added that **only** the **industrial proletariat** (factory workers) was capable of articulating the grievances of this whole class in the revolutionary direction. This could be done only by transcending local economic grievances and narrow trade unionism. For this, there was a need of a national level political organisation. Only such an organisation could raise the level of political consciousness of the workers by transforming the wage labour class into a revolutionary proletariat class capable of staging a successful revolution.

In this work, **Lenin argued** that in conditions prevailing in Russia there was need of a Communist Party which could act as a Vanguard of the Proletariat. (**Stalin** further elaborated this idea when he argued that a working class without a Communist Party was like an army without the General staff).

Lenin did not emphasis the need of such a **Communist Party** in **Russia,** he also added that this **Vanguard Party** should consist of or at least be led by whole time professional revolutionaries. Only then successful revolution could be brought about. In fact, the task which **Marx** had assigned to the proletariat class in staging a successful revolution got transferred to the Communist Party as the vanguard of this class.

Lenin's vanguard thesis was criticized by several of his **contemporaries**, particularly by a Polish Marxist **Rosa Luxembourg.** She argued that this would place the working class in tutelage of the party. She also pointed out that due to Lenin's vanguard thesis, the workers would lose all their initiative and become mere tools in the hands of the party.

Democratic Centralism

Having made the **Communist Party** as the **vanguard** of the proletariat, **Lenin advocated** a certain type of organizational structure for the party. His thesis is popularly known as 'democratic centralism'. To put it in simple words, democratic centralism consisted of **two elements**: democracy and centralism.

It meant that the hierarchical structure of the *Communist Party* should be such that each higher organ of the party should be elected by the lower organ and all the party matters should initially discuss freely at all the levels of the organisation, from the lowest to the highest.

However, once a decision has been taken by the highest organ it should be imposed strictly on all the lower organs & all of them must abide by it. While theoretically democratic centralism has democracy as well as centralism, in actual practice the Party became less & less democratic & more & more centralized. Like his Vanguard thesis, **Lenin's** views on democratic centralism were also criticized by several of his contemporaries.

Imperialism [Q.4 of Book]

Marx in his analysis of **capitalism** had argued that in the task of <u>overthrowing autocracy & feudalism</u>, the bourgeoisie plays a revolutionary role and brings about **democracy** and **capitalism**. This is called the bourgeois democratic revolution. It puts the bourgeoisie into power.

Under the rule of the bourgeoisie, capitalism would develop further. **Finally**, it would reach a stage where the class contradiction between the bourgeoisie and the proletariat would become very sharp. This would create conditions for a proletarian socialist revolution which would mark the demise of capitalism.

Weakest Link of the Chain

The success of the **Bolshevik Revolution** in a capitalistically under-developed country like **Russia** in **1917** raised two new problems for Lenin. The first problem was to reconcile and interpret this revolution in Marxian terms. Lenin did so by inventing 'the weakest link of the chain' argument.

It meant that **Tsarist Russia** where capitalism was not yet fully developed constituted the weakest link of the imperialist chain and strategically it is quite appropriate to break the chain at its weakest rather than at its strongest point. In fact, this whole idea is also **implicit in Marx**. Marx had argued that with the development of capitalism, the bourgeoisie becomes **stronger & stronger**.

The **second problem** for Lenin was more serious. Since the **revolution** had occurred in **Tsarist Russia** where capitalism was still unripe, the problem was to **draw a plan** for building a socialist state. The problem got further compounded because Marx in his writings had given a very sketchy picture of the socialist stage and had not explained in detail how a socialist society would come about.

The **Capitalist State**, according to Lenin, emerged as an organ of class rule. It was a special organisation of force and violence fix the exploitation of the working class. This capitalist state had to be replaced by a socialist state.

In his **State and Revolution**, Lenin offered some outlines of his strategy to built such a **socialist state in Russia**. He argued that the bureaucratic military state was to be replaced by soviets modelled on the lines of the Paris Commune. Moreover, he did not subscribe fully to the **Marxist notion** of withering away of the state.

Spontaneity Element gives way to Selectivity of Time & Place

As pointed out earlier, Lenin assigned the task of staging a successful proletarian revolution to the communist party as the vanguard of the proletariat. This amounted lo some deviation from the Marxian position. Marx had expressed considerable Faith in the revolutionary potential of the working class. But in Lenin's argument, the spontaneity element inherent in Marx gave way to selectivity of time and place.

Lenin was critical of the view expressed by the Mensheviks (minority faction in the party) that revolutionaries should wait for the development of spontaneous revolutionary action of the masses. He argued that without strong leadership from outside its ranks, the working class could never rise beyond trade unionism. He considered such trade unionism reformist rather than revolutionary.

It amounted to saying that the leadership of the Communist Party would decide where and when the revolution is to be attempted. In other words, the agenda of revolution would be decided by the party and not by the workers. This view of Lenin was criticised by some of his contemporaries, particularly Rosa Luxemberg.

She argued that since the decision about time, place and strategy of the revolution was to be decided by the Communist Party, the spontaneity element of a revolution which is inherent in Marx would give way to selectivity of time and place. This, she further added, would blunt the self-emancipatory efforts of the working class.

MAO TSE-TUNG (NOW MAO ZEDONG) (1893 – 1976)

Born at Shaoshan in Hunan province of China in 1893 (December 26) Mao is the second Marxist revolutionary (Lenin being the first) who brought about a successful revolution in a backward country like China.

Moreovcr, he did so primarily with the help of the peasantry - a class which, Marx thought, had no revolutionary potential. Even Lenin had not placed much faith in the peasant class. Mao, like Lenin, was both a practitioner of Marxism & also its theoretician.

After a little formal education, he joined the arrny of Hunan province during the 1911 revolution led by Kuomintang(KMT), a bourgeois nationalist party of Sun Yat Sen. Soon after the success of the KMT revolution, he moved to Changsha (Capital of Hunan) and later lo Peking (Now Beijing).

There he came under the influence of the radical Marxist leader Li Dazhao who arranged a job for him in the University Library. However, he left the job and returned to Changsha & became active in the Communist Party of China (CPC).

By 1927, the relations between the KMT and the CPC became so bitter that the KMT decided to hit at the communists. After this break between the KMT and the CPC, Mao was asked to organise a rebellion of Hunan peasants.

Peasant Revolution

Mao is a great innovator in his own right. He modified Marxism Leninism by relying heavily on the peasantry's revolutionary potential. It need to be renumbered that Marx has treated the peasantry with some degree of contempt.

For the most part, peasantry for him was conservative & reactionary; it was no more than a bag of potatoes unable to make a revolution.

Mao's fundamental contribution, therefore, was to bring about a successful revolution in China mainly with the help of the peasantry. More than anything else, his revolutionary model became relevant for several Afro-Asian peasant societies.

Secondly, Mao in his cultural revolution phase drew some lessons from the course of post-revolutionary reconstruction in the Soviet Union and warned (like Milovan Djilas) against the emergence of the new bourgeois class who were beneficiaries of the transitional period.

Contradictions

In Marxist theory, the main vehicle of all changes in society is contradiction. **Mao** further elaborated this idea.

For him, contradictions or the unity of opposites (thesis and anti-thesis) leading to a higher level and transforming quantity to quality (synthesis) was the fundamental law of historical development.

But he did not fully endorse the Marxist position on contradiction. It may be mentioned that Marx, in his writings, seems to have used the terms contradictions and antagonisms almost interchangeably.

Contradictions between the various communist parties were non-antagonistic, but contradictions between the Chinese people and the comprador bourgeoisie were antagonistic. Contradictions between the socialist and the capitalist camp were antagonistic. Contradictions between colonial countries and imperialism were antagonistic.

On Practice

This elaboration of contradictions led Mao to expound his epistemology or theory of knowledge. In his famous essay titled, **On Practice** (1973) **Mao** argued that all knowledge of real world comes to us through concrete investigation & empirical analysis. He opposed to mere book learning or intuitive theorising.

For example, if one wanted to understand the Chinese society, then one must understand its class structure, its pattern of land ownership and the impact of imperialism on the local **economy of China**. Theory without continuous reference to empirical reality would become a mere dogma.

However, he visualized **two** stages in the understanding of empirical reality: The **Perceptual** stage, and The **Conceptual** Stage. At the perceptual stage, we only get the impression of reality through our senses.

This sense perception has to be compounded into conceptual knowledge. But having seen this reality, one has to understand it in terms of different strata's of peasantry: landless, marginal, small, middle & big farmers etc., that is the conceptual stage.

United Front and New Democracy

Mao realized that the **peasantry in China** was **not strong enough** to <u>win the revolutionary struggle</u> against imperialism and feudalism. Therefore, it was necessary to seek the help of the other classes of Chinese society.

It was in this context that **Mao** *emphasized the concept* of a **United Front**. It was seen as <u>an alliance between</u> different partners who laid some common interest like opposition to imperialism. The nature of such a United Front would depend on the historical situation.

Its object would be to pursue the resolution of the principal contradiction. Such a United Front strategy was employed by Mao by establishing the alliance of Chinese peasantry with the proletariat, the petty bourgeoisie and even the national bourgeoisie.

It also intended the non-party elements among the Chinese intellectuals. The United front had to be a broad alliance of the Chinese people against Japanese imperialism and western powers.

In pursuance of his <u>United Front</u> strategy, **Mao** gave a call in **1940** for a <u>new democratic republic of China</u>. It was to be a state under the joint dictatorship of several classes. In **1945**, he proposed a state system which is called New Democracy.

While the united front consisted of an overwhelming majority of the Chinese people, the leading position in the alliance had to be in the hands of the working class. It was a combination of two aspects - democracy for the people and dictatorship over the 'enemies of the people' or the 'running dogs of imperialism'. In fact, he combined Marxism and nationalism.

Solved IGNOU Book Exercise & Solved Past 8 Attempts Questions

❏ IGNOU BOOK EXERCISE

1. What is the main intellectual contribution of 'early' Marx? How does 'early' Marx differ from 'later' Marx?   (Dec-20)

Answer by India Ebook: The Answer is marked in the Summary Concept of this Unit.

5. Describe Mao's analysis of classes in the Chinese society.

Answer by India Ebook: Mao was born at Shaoshan in Hunan province of China in 1893 (December 26) Mao is the second Marxist revolutionary (Lenin being the first) who brought about a successful revolution in a backward country like China.

Moreover, he did so primarily with the help of the peasantry - a class which, Marx thought, had no revolutionary potential. Even Lenin had not placed much faith in the peasant class. Mao, like Lenin, was both a practitioner of Marxism & also its theoretician.

After a little formal education, he joined the arrny of Hunan province during the 1911 revolution led by Kuomintang(KMT), a bourgeois nationalist party of Sun Yat Sen. Soon after the success of the KMT revolution, he moved to Changsha (Capital of Hunan) and later lo Peking (Now Beijing).

There he came under the influence of the radical Marxist leader Li Dazhao who arranged a job for him in the University Library. However, he left the job and returned to Changsha & became active in the Communist Party of China (CPC).

By 1927, the relations between the KMT and the CPC became so bitter that the KMT decided to hit at the communists. After this break between the KMT and the CPC, Mao was asked to organise a rebellion of Hunan peasants.

Mao is a great innovator in his own right. He modified Marxism Leninism by relying heavily on the peasantry's revolutionary potential. It need to be renumbered that Marx has treated the peasantry with some degree of contempt.

For the most part, peasantry for him was conservative & reactionary; it was no more than a bag of potatoes unable to make a revolution.

Mao's fundamental contribution, therefore, was to bring about a successful revolution in China mainly with the help of the peasantry. More than anything else, his revolutionary model became relevant for several Afro-Asian peasant societies.

Secondly, Mao in his cultural revolution phase drew some lessons from the course of post-revolutionary reconstruction in the Soviet Union and warned (like Milovan Djilas) against the emergence of the new bourgeois class who were beneficiaries of the transitional period.

6. What has been Mao's contribution to the theory of contradictions?

Answer by India Ebook: In Marxist theory, the main vehicle of all changes in society is contradiction. **Mao** further elaborated this idea.

For him, contradictions or the unity of opposites (thesis and anti-thesis) leading to a higher level and transforming quantity to quality (synthesis) was the fundamental law of historical development.

But he did not fully endorse the Marxist position on contradiction. It may be mentioned that Marx, in his writings, seems to have used the terms contradictions and antagonisms almost interchangeably.

Contradictions between the various communist parties were non-antagonistic, but contradictions between the Chinese people and the comprador bourgeoisie were antagonistic. Contradictions between the socialist and the capitalist camp were antagonistic. Contradictions between colonial countries and imperialism were antagonistic.

This elaboration of contradictions led Mao to expound his epistemology or theory of knowledge. In his famous essay titled, **On Practice** (1973) **Mao** argued that all knowledge of real world comes to us through concrete investigation & empirical analysis. He opposed to mere book learning or intuitive theorising.

For example, if one wanted to understand the Chinese society, then one must understand its class structure, its pattern of land ownership and the impact of imperialism on the local **economy of China**. Theory without continuous reference to empirical reality would become a mere dogma.

However, he visualized **two** stages in the understanding of empirical reality: The **Perceptual** stage, and The **Conceptual** Stage. At the perceptual stage, we only get the impression of reality through our senses.

This sense perception has to be compounded into conceptual knowledge. But having seen this reality, one has to understand it in terms of different strata's of peasantry: landless, marginal, small, middle & big farmers etc., that is the conceptual stage.

7. Comment on Mao's notion of New Democracy.

Answer by India Ebook: Mao realized that the **peasantry in China** was **not strong enough** to win the revolutionary struggle against imperialism and feudalism. Therefore, it was necessary to seek the help of the other classes of Chinese society.

It was in this context that **Mao** *emphasized the concept* of a **United Front**. It was seen as an alliance between different partners who Iaid some common interest like opposition to imperialism. The nature of such a United Front would depend on the historical situation.

Its object would be to pursue the resolution of the principal contradiction. Such a United Front strategy was employed by Mao by establishing the alliance of Chinese peasantry with the proletariat, the petty bourgeoisie and even the national bourgeoisie.

It also intended the non-party elements among the Chinese intellectuals. The United front had to be a broad alliance of the Chinese people against Japanese imperialism and western powers.

In pursuance of his United Front strategy, **Mao** gave a call in **1940** for a new democratic republic of China. It was to be a state under the joint dictatorship of several classes. In **1945**, he proposed a state system which is called New Democracy.

While the united front consisted of an overwhelming majority of the Chinese people, the leading position in the alliance had to be in the hands of the working class. It was a combination of two aspects - democracy for the people and dictatorship over the 'enemies of the people' or the 'running dogs of imperialism'. In fact, he combined Marxism and nationalism.

❏ PAST 8 ATTEMPTS IGNOU QUESTIONS

Dec 2020: E-1: Describe the contribution of Karl Marx to Political Theory.

Answer by India Ebook: Exact same as **Q.1** of Above.

Dec 2019: E-2: Write a short note on Marx's Theory of Surplus.

Answer by India Ebook: First Give a Brief Introduction about Marx… then…..Refer the Whole Topic of Marx's Surplus Theory Above.

Dec 2018: E-1: Discuss Lenin's contribution to bring communist revolution in Russia.

Answer by India Ebook: Refer the Whole Topic of LENIN Above.

19. MPS-001: UNIT-19: Marxism-II Lukacs, Gramsci, Frankfurt School

- Introduction
- Georg Lukacs (1885 – 1971)
  - Rejection of Dialectical Materialism
  - Denial of Lenin's Vanguard Thesis
  - Relation of Subject & Object
- Antonio Gramsci (1891 – 1937) : Notion of Hegemony; Role of Intellectuals; Philosophy of Praxis; Relation between Base & Super-Structure & Notion of Historic Bloc
- Frankfurt School (or Critical Theory) : Opposition to all Forms of Domination; Critique of Orthodox Marxism; In Search of Emancipation
- Exercise & Past 8 Attempts Questions

IGNOU Book Exercise & Past 8 Attempts Questions - IMPORTANT

❏ IGNOU BOOK EXERCISE

3. What is meant by the Frankfurt School? What critique of liberal and socialist societies did it offer? **(Dec 2018)**

Answer by India Ebook: Frankfurt School refers to a group of philosophers who were together at the **Frankfurt Institute for Social Research** during the **1920s** and **30s**. Prominent members of the school were Horkheimer, Adorno, Pollock, Eric Fromm, Neumann and Herbert Marcuse. All of them, one way or the other, contributed to the Marxist theory. Of course, there were differences among them on many issues, but there is <u>some common streak</u> which emerges from their writings. Their view also came to be called **Critical Theory**. They were all critical of all forms of domination and exploitation in society.

They were also critical of they **Stalinist variety of socialism**. They argued that Marxism was <u>not a closed system</u>. They are more concerned with cultural and ideological issues than with political economy which is the core of orthodox Marxism.

Opposition to all Forms of Domination

At the very outset, you must understand the context in which they wrote and the issues which bothered them. They wrote in a period which was marked by the rise of **Nazism** (in Germany) and **Fascism** (in Italy). Moreover, the rise of **Stalinism** in the **Soviet Union** with its totalitarian thrust was a cause of serious concern for them. They were also aware of the failure of Communist movements in Western Europe.

Through critical analysis of such ideologies, they wanted to trace the hidden roots of domination in them. By doing so, they tried to create true consciousness among the masses and prepare them for revolutionary action. Thus, their goal like Marx is revolutionary transformation of society, but in a different way.

Critique of Orthodox Marxism

The Frankfurt School tried to offer a critique of some of the notions of orthodox Marxism which had acquired repressive and authoritarian intent in the Soviet Union. Some of them even went to the extent of saying that Marxism is not adequate to explain trends like bureaucratization.

Like Lukacs and Gramsci, they also questioned the Marxian doctrine of historical materialism which tries to explain all stages in historical developments in economic terms. They argued that it underplays the role or human subjectivity. In fact, they tried to show that this 'determinist' thrust (economic base determining everything) was the result of Marx's acceptance of positivist methodology of natural sciences.

In Search of Emancipation

The central concern in the writings of the Frankfurt school is domination and authority. They argued that in liberal as well as socialist societies, domination and authority are justified in the name of reason which they call instrumental rationality. In fact, it is the result of the application of the positivist methods of natural sciences to social sciences.

In natural sciences, we study the physical phenomenon with a view to control and regulate it, but in human sciences the object of study of society should not be to control and regulate human beings, but to emancipate them from all sorts of bondages. All socio-cultural practices in western as well as eastern societies are aimed at stabilizing the system of domination. They are also critical of authoritarian family structures and the socialization processes in education. They stand for sexual liberation as well.

❑ PAST 8 ATTEMPTS IGNOU QUESTIONS

June 2022: E-1: Elaborate Antonio Gramsci's views on the base-superstructure inter-relationship.

Answer by India Ebook: Gramsci was born in a poor family in **Sardina** which was the poorest region of **Italy**. His father was arrested for embezzlement when **Gramsci** was a small child and sentenced to **5** years imprisonment. In his absence, the family lived in utter poverty because of which Gramsci suffered physical deformity and became a hunchback.

After some elementary education, Gramsci started **working** in an office. In **1911** he won a scholarship and joined **Turin University**. At Turin, he noticed that there was a lot of difference in the standard of living in the rural areas of Italy and its cities. While at the university, he got associated with the **Italian Socialist Party**.

By and by he was attracted to **Marxist** ideas. He was also influenced by Corce's emphasis on the role of culture and thought in the development of history. It was this idea of Corce which provided the historical framework within which **Gramsci** carried out his adaptation of Marxian ideas.

It **was in 1914-15** when **Gramsci** attended some lectures on Marxism that he got interested in the problem of **relations between the base and the super-structure**. For Marx, the economic order of society constituted the base and the political order constituted the super structure. The nature of super structure depended on the nature of the economic base.

Gramsci modified this Marxian position. He talked of a historic bloc. The historic bloc for Gramsci was a situation when both objective and subjective forces combine to produce a revolutionary situation. It is a situation when the old order is collapsing and there are also people with will and historical insight to take advantage of this situation.

The union of base and super-structure, material conditions and ideologies, constitute the historic bloc. In other words, even when the material forces have reached a point where revolution is possible, its occurrence would depend on correct intellectual analysis in order to have a rational reflection of the contradictions of the structure.

For Gramsci, dialectics means three things:

i) interaction between the intellectuals (party leaders) and the masses;

ii) explanation of historical developments in terms of thesis, anti-thesis and synthesis;

iii) the relation between the sub-structure and super-structure.

Thus, it is the moment when sub-structure and super-structure interact on each other to produce a historic bloc.

20. MPS-001: UNIT-20: Socialism

- ➤ Introduction; The Doctrine of Social Progress, Individualism and Capitalism
- ➤ Socialism: Meaning & Early Strands; Karl Marx & Socialism
- ➤ Critiques of Marxism and Democratic Socialism

Solved IGNOU Book Exercise & Solved Past 8 Attempts Questions

❑ **IGNOU BOOK EXERCISE**

5. Examine the critiques of Marxism.

Answer by India Ebook: It is important to look at a two way challenge to **Marxism** that emerged at the end of the **19**th century. This took the shape, during the course of the **20**th century, to **evolutionary** or "**democratic**" socialism.

When the **workers' revolution** did not take place, as **Marx** had foreseen that it soon will, there emerged strong reservations about Marxism as a body of doctrines. One who expressed this in systematic terms was a long time **German Marxist Eduard Bernstein**. In a book entitled Evolutionary Socialism, he elaborated a wholly different route to and tactics for achieving a socialist society.

The other line of development took shape not because revolution did not come about, but because a large group of British Socialists had intrinsic reservations about Marxism. They thought that some of its goals and methods and tactics will result in authoritarian, despotic politics.

They took exceptions to goals like the dictatorship of the proletariat, class warfare, violent overthrow of capitalism etc. To further an alternative way of achieving socialism together with strengthening democracy, leading socialists formed themselves into a **Fabian Society** in the middle of the **1880's** and this version eventually came to be known as **Fabian Socialism**.

Bernstein argued that the wages of workers are **not falling** but are, relatively rising because the rate of profit is not, as **Marx** argued, declining and therefore, the expected impoverishments of the workers and the consequent uprising will not come about. Rather, the workers would get more and more integrated into the capitalist system.

Hence, the need is to work within the capitalist system by accepting its institutional framework of parliament, elections, open political activity and thereby, striving to improve the condition of the working class. The class of workers has already become the majority and by proper organisation, it is now possible to win a majority in parliament and strive towards socialist ideals. In short, they declared that there is no need for revolution.

Through the different routes, these two critiques of Marxism came to similar conclusions, which can be stated as the core tenets of "democratic socialism". Four of these deserve a mention.

First, socialism is not as Marx thought a historical necessity or inevitable but a moral need for the good of humanity.

Secondly, that in a transition to socialism it is not only the working class, but the entire people who will play a part; working class as the predominant part of the world will no doubt be strategic.

Thirdly, the route to socialism will not be through a violent rupture, as Marx thought, but would be by a gradual ascent. In this, by degrees, through closely interconnected legislative measures, structure of socialist economy can be put in place.

Lastly, the state will remain an institution of strategic importance. Through a series of nationalisation measures, the state will ensure that the private ownership of the means of production will be socialised; that is, different forms of state & cooperative ownerships in industry & public services like health care, education, electricity, railways, etc., will be instituted.

Socialism is no simple, monolithic doctrine like Soviet communism was. It represents a variation upon variation, a multiplicity of viewpoints but, as we have seen, sharing some core assumptions and presuppositions.

6. Describe the salient features of Democratic Socialism. (June 2020, Dec 2018)

Answer by India Ebook: Almost same as **Q.5** of the above.

❑ PAST 8 ATTEMPTS IGNOU QUESTIONS

June 2020: E-1: Write a note on the teachers' democratic socialism.

Answer by India Ebook: Exact same as **Q.6** of Above.

Dec 2018: E-2: Write short notes on: (c) Democratic Socialism.

Answer by India Ebook: Exact same as **Q.6** of Above.

21. MPS-001: UNIT-21: Conservatism

- ➤ Introduction; Meaning of Conservatism
- ➤ Numerous Uses of the Term Conservatism
- ➤ Temperamental Conservatism
- ➤ Situational Conservatism
- ➤ Political Conservatism
- ➤ Conservatism: Its Characteristics Features – History & Tradition; Human Imperfection, Prejudice & Reason; Organic Society, Liberty & Equality; Authority & Power; Property & Life; Relation & Morality
- ➤ Some Representative Conservatives
- ➤ Exercise & Past 8 Attempts Questions

INTRODUCTION

Conservatism is an <u>ideology of conservation</u>. It developed essentially as a **reaction against the growing pace** of political and economic changes especially in the West. This is one reason that any use of the word 'conservatism' resists change.

As a philosophy, it **defends** the **values of hierarchy**, **tradition** and order against pressures generated by industrialisation and represented by the political challenges of liberalism and socialism.

That is why there is a basic distinction among the leftists and socialists, libertarians and conservatives. The leftists and the socialists are the party of bureaucracy (i.e., hard-core communists); libertarians, of markets; and conservatives, of tradition.

Some **principles** of Conservatism as given by **Clinton Rossiter**, are:

[Q.2 of Book... 1st Part]

(i) The existence of a universal moral order sanctioned and supported by organised religion;

(ii) The obstinately imperfect nature of men in which unreason and sinfulness lurk always behind the curtain of civilized behavior;

(iii) The natural inequality of men in most qualities of mind, body and character;

(iv) The necessity of social classes and orders, and the consequent folly of attempts at levelling by force of law;

(v) The primary role of private property in the pursuit of personal liberty and the defense of social order;

(vi) The uncertainty of progress, and the recognition that prescription is the chief method of such progress as a society may achieve;

(vii) The need for a ruling and serving aristocracy,

(viii) The limited search of human reason and the consequent importance of traditions, institutions, symbols, rituals & even prejudices;

(ix) The fallibility and potential tyranny of majority rule, & the consequent desirability of diffusing, limiting and balancing political power.

MEANING OF CONSERVATISM {Q.1 of Book}

The term 'conservative' has a variety of meanings. It may refer to a person with a moderate or cautious behavior, or a life style that is conventional, even conformist, or a fear of, or refusal to change. Conservatism is an ideology which opposes more than it favours.

Andrew Haywood ('Political Ideologies') rightly says that: "There is, for example, some truth in the belief that conservatives have a clearer understanding of what they oppose than what they favour".

Conservatism is a negative philosophy which preaches resistance to or at-least wary suspicion of change: it is, therefore, a defence of the status quo. In this sense, conservatism is a political attitude rather than an ideology. People may be considered to be 'conservative' when they resist change, without subscribing to a conservative political creed.

De Kirk lists **six canons** of **conservative thought:**

[Q.2 of Book..........2nd Part]

1) A "belief in a body of natural law which rules society and conscience."

2) A love of variety & the mystery of human existence, as opposed to narrowing uniformity, egalitarianism & utilitarianism.

3) A "conviction that civilized society requires orders and classes as opposed to a 'classless' society: equality in the judgement of God and before courts of law. Equality of condition means equality in servitude and boredom."

4) "Freedom and prosperity are inseparable, or else government becomes the master of all,"

5) A "faith in prescription, for customs, conventions & old prescriptions are checks upon anarchy & man's lust for power."

6) "Change may not be good reform, a statesman's chief virtue is prudence."

NUMEROUS USES OF THE TERM CONSERVATISM

It is much easier to locate the historical context i.e., period between 750 and 1850 as a response to the rapid series of changes in which conservatism evolved than to specify what is or what the conservatives believe.

Sometimes, conservatism means outright opposition to all and every change; at others, it means an attempt to reconstruct a form of society which existed in an earlier period. Still at other times, it appears to be primarily a political reaction and secondarily, a body of ideas.

Temperamental Conservatism

Conservatism, by one definition, denotes a 'natural' and culture-determined disposition to resist dislocating changes in a customary pattern of living and working. According to **Rossiter**, "It effectively is, a temperament or psychological stance, a cluster of traits that are on daily display by most men in all societies." He lists the **important elements** of _conservative temperament_ as:

(a) **habit** (the enormous fly-wheel of society and its most precious conservative agent),

(b) **inertia** (a force that often seems to be as powerful in the social world as in the physical),

(c) **fear** (especially fear of the unexpected, the irregular and the uncomfortable), and

(d) **emulation** (a product of both fear of alienation from the group and a craving for its approval).

So understood, one may speak, with propriety, of the conservatism of the poor, of the aged and of the ignorant. "At the same time", **Rossitter writes**, "one must assign a high value to the conservative temperament in the pattern of social survival and even of social progress".

Situational Conservatism

Conservatism, by a **second definition**, related to the **first**, is an <u>attitude of opposition</u> to disruptive changes in the social, economic, legal, religious, political or cultural order. "It describes", **Rossiter** clarifies, "somewhat less crudely and somewhat more effectively, a pattern of social behaviour, a cluster of principles and prejudices that are on daily display by many men in all developed societies."

Situational conservatism is **not confined** only to the **well-to-do**; it extends to all levels of people who lament change in the **status quo**.

It is unfortunate that **both** temperamental conservatism and situational conservatism-tend to be equated to authoritarianism, obscurantism, racism, fascism, alienation, maladjustment, and **'the closed mind'** studies are needed before these elements are linked to either of conservatism.

Political Conservatism

Conservatism, by still another definition, is the <u>aspirations and activities,</u> most of them defensive rather than creative, of parties and movements that celebrate inherited patterns of morality and tested institutions that oppose the reforming plans of the moderate left and the schemes of the extreme left.

Political conservatism is a **phenomenon** which is universal of organised society, and essentially, the defense of a going society. **Reaction** is <u>not conservatism</u>. It is the position of men who sigh for more intensively than they celebrate the present and who feel that a retreat back into it is worth trying.

CONSERVATISM: ITS CHARACTERISTIC FEATURES

"The desire to conserve", the words which <u>**Edmund Burke**</u> used, is the underlying theme of conservative ideology, though it is not the sole objective which conservatives of all shades seek to attain. Authoritarian conservatism has often been reactionary; it either refuses to yield to change or attempts to turn the clock back.

Revolutionary conservatism may use the term radical conservatism and tends to **regain** or **re-establish** or **argue** for a conservative fabric of revolutionary character. The **characteristic features** of conservatism, as evolved in different forms and conveying the fundamentals of conservatism can be identified.

History and Tradition {Q.3 and Q.4 of Book}

The role of history and tradition is basic to **any type** of conservatism. History, reduced to its essentials, is nothing but experience. It is deductive thought in matters of human relationship, Legitimacy is the work of history.

The **correctness of history** or of **experience** for that matter is a persisting conservative emphasis. This has been shown by Burke, Rourke, Oakeshott and Voegelin, to mention a few. **Social reality** can be understood through a historical approach: "We cannot know where we are, much less where we are going, until we know where we have been. That is the bedrock position of the conservative philosophy of history". (**'Conservatism: Dream and Reality'**).

History is **represented** in traditions, and traditions constitute an important component of history. As such, a central theme of conservatism is, with regard to history, its defence of traditions, its desire to maintain established customs and institutions.

Human Imperfection, Prejudice & Reason

Conservatism is a philosophy of human imperfection; the roots of man's basis lay more in prejudice than in reason. As against the liberals, who think of human beings as moral, rational and social, the conservatives regards men, both imperfect and un-perfectible.

Human beings, the conservatives believe, are dependent creatures, always fearing isolation and instability, and therefore, always seek safety, security and what is familiar, ready always to sacrifice liberty for social order.

Reason stems from knowledge that is learnt than imparted. The conservatives are of the opinion that imparted knowledge leads to abstractions, abstract knowledge, and for human beings, it is too complicated to be fully grasped.

Organic Society, Liberty and Equality

The conservative view of society is an organic view of society: the individuals don't & cannot exist outside society, but they are **rooted** in society, & **belong** to it; they are parts of social groups & these groups provide individuals' lives with security & meaning.

The conservative's view of liberty is not 'leaving the individual alone', but is one where there is willing acceptance of social obligations & ties. For the conservatives, liberty is primarily 'doing one's duty'. When the parents, for example, advise their children to behave in a particular way, they do not constrain their liberty, but they are providing a basis for the liberty the children would enjoy when they grow up.

The conservative view of society is one that is a living thing, an organism whose parts are neither equal nor the same, work together and make the human body function properly; each part of the organic society (i.e., family, government, a factory) plays a particular role in sustaining and maintaining the health of society.

Authority and Power

Authority and power, in the sense they are used, have much in **common for a conservative**. Power is used by one who is authorised to exercise it and it is the legitimate act to get what one wills.

In an organic society, order has to be maintained: so **power** is an essential component of an organic society. In an hierarchical system, there are different levels; so authority became necessary. Power and authority are the important concepts in conservative philosophy. These, in no sense, constitute an obstacle to what conservatives think about liberty.

The conservatives believe that authority, like society, develops naturally; power emerges from functions. Authority and power, the conservatives strongly feel, develop from natural society. These are natural because they are rooted in the nature of society and all social institutions.

Within **school**, authority or power is, and in fact, should be exercised by the teacher; in the **work place**, by the employer; and in the **society**, by the government. The conservatives say that authority is necessary because it is beneficial, as every one needs the guidance, support and security of knowing where the people stand and what is expected of them. That is why all the conservatives emphasise leadership and discipline.

No conservative believes in **equality**, in social equality at that. They think that people are born unequally in the sense that: talents and skills are distributed unequally: unequal should not be treated equally. Conservatism adores power in so far as it helps establish order in society.

It admires authority because it is authority through which order is established in society. Conservatives favour an authoritarian and all-powerful state. Public order & the moral fabric of society can be maintained through the power & authority of the state.

Property and Life

Property, for conservatives, possesses a deep and mystical significance. The conservatives hold the view that property has a range of psychological and social advantages: it provides security; gives people a sense of confidence; promotes social values.

As such, the conservatives want that property must be safeguarded from disorder and lawlessness. They say that the property owners have a stake in society. They have an interest in maintaining law and order. Property ownership promotes the conservative values of respecting the law, authority and social order.

Religion and Morality

Conservatism is, indeed, unique among major ideologies in its emphasis on religion and morality. Irrespective of denomination, all the conservatives including Hegel, Haller and Coleridge made religion, and therefore morality, a keynote of state and society.

The conservative support for religion and morality rests on the well-founded belief that human beings, once they get adrift from major orthodoxy, are likely to suffer some measure of derangement, of loss of equilibrium. "Religion", Burke wrote to his son, "is man's fastness in an otherwise incomprehensible and thereby hostile world".

Religion is a spiritual phenomenon. But at the same time, it is an essential social element as well. For the conservatives, these exists a close relationship between religion and conservatism, for religion provides society a moral fabric.

SOME REPRESENTATIVE CONSERVATISM [Q.5 of Book]

It is only by way of completing an argument for conservatism that an attempt is being made to mention a few, and among them, two major representative conservatives; Burke and **Oakeshott.**

Oakeshott's plea for traditionalism, as an aspect of his conservatism in politics, morals and life, in general, proceeds logically from his critique of rationalism. According to Oakeshott, the ideological style of politics (i.e., the rationalist style) is a confused style, for ideology in the rationalist scheme, as he thinks, is merely an abridgement, an index.

So, Oalceshott's answer is that the only style, one should adopt and pursue, is the traditional one. Political activity, Oakeshott affirms, cannot spring but from the existing traditions of behavior and the form that it takes is the amendment of existing arrangements by exploring and pursuing what is implied in them.

All activity, for him, therefore, is traditional in nature. Every idea, every ideal, every ideology, even the most revolutionary, as described by Oakeshott, is traditional, always an index, an abridgement of traditional manner of attending to the arrangements of society.

Tradition, Oakeshott feels, is not a fixed manner of dong thing, but is flow of sympathy. Every political activity, therefore, is a consequential activity for him, the pursuit of intimation as he fondly calls it. This means that political activity is what political activity actually is and not what it can be or it ought to be. It is what it succeeds actually in doing. All those who indulge; Oakeshott says, in revolutionary or idealistic actions indulge only in self-deception.

Like Burke, Oakeshott regards society as a conversation rather than an argument. Tradition, according to Oakeshott, is described as anything under the sun.

Solved IGNOU Book Exercise & Solved Past 8 Attempts Questions

❏ IGNOU BOOK EXERCISE

1. Explain the meaning of conservatism. In how many **major senses** the word 'conservatism' is used?

Answer by India Ebook: The Answer is marked in the Summary Concept of this Unit.

2. What are, in your view, **principles and canons** of conservatism?

Answer by India Ebook: The Answer is marked in the Summary Concept of this Unit.

3. Describe briefly the **characteristic features** of conservatism.

Answer by India Ebook: The Answer is marked in the Summary Concept of this Unit.

4. What did Write a note on **Edmund Burke** as a conservative thinker.

Answer by India Ebook: The Answer is marked in the Summary Concept of this Unit.

5. What is meant How does **Michael Oakeshott** defend traditionalism? Explain in detail.

Answer by India Ebook: The Answer is marked in the Summary Concept of this Unit.

❏ PAST 8 ATTEMPTS IGNOU QUESTIONS

June 2020: E-1: Describe the silent features of Conservatism.

Answer by India Ebook: Exact same as **Q.3** of Above.

22. MPS-001: UNIT-22: Fundamentalism

- ➢ Introduction
- ➢ Meaning of Fundamentalism
- ➢ Ideology and Fundamentalism
- ➢ Core Characteristics of Fundamentalism
- ➢ Identity of Secular and Religious Fundamentalism
- ➢ The Fundamentalist Mind
- ➢ Comparing Fundamentalism

Solved IGNOU Book Exercise & Solved Past 8 Attempts Questions

❑ **IGNOU BOOK EXERCISE**

5. **Compare briefly the Hindu, Islamic and Christian fundamentalisms.**

Answer by India Ebook: Religions like ideologies vary. They differ in their potential for becoming fundamentalistic. The more monolithic a religion or ideology is, the more are the chances of it turning to fundamentalism.

Islam and the evangelical Protestant strand of Christianity are monolithic religions; they believe that there is just one God; they are also dogmatic; they believe it is possible to express his (God's) nature and will in specific propositions: both these things are the necessary pre-conditions for fundamentalism.

Hinduism, as a religion, in the context of **Islam** and **Protestant Christianity** as they are, is <u>less monolithic</u> and dogmatic & hence, less fundamentalistic. There are a number of reasons for that: there is diffuseness in Hinduism, different deities, a variety of gods. So diffused is the society as well: a variety of traditions, groups, sects.

It may be, **Bruce** says, "better described **not as a religion**, but as a <u>loose collection</u> of **religions**: that of the Shaivites, the Vnishnavas, the Shalcras, the Smartas, & others - that share some common themes but they tolerate a huge variety of expressions of these themes. As those expression can vary from village to village & caste to caste, there is a little scope for enforcing conformity, criticising laxity, or vigorously rejecting moderate reconstructions of the tradition. Instead of the single

Bible or Quran, there are a large numbers of holy books and holy traditions."

Within itself, **revivalistic attempts** have been at work in **Hinduism**: sometimes in the forms of Buddhism, Jainism or Sikhism at an early period of history or in the forms of Brahmo Samaj, Arya Samaj, Ramakrishna Mission or Ved-Samaj during the greater part of the **19th century**.

Protestantism and Islam have much in common. Their potentials are the same: both can generate fundamentalism; their aims are similar: each wishes to assert the primacy of its religious belief systems and the patterns of behaviour each belief system requires.

But both differ in their methods. The **Islamic fundamentalists** believe that coercion is proper; most of them believe that it is necessary as well, while others feel that it is required, declaring 'jihad' literally.

The **Protestant fundamentalists** do not believe so. Christ preached against the old law of 'eye for an eye' and instead recommended to offer another cheek to the person who has already hit the first check. 'Though radical Protestants have created militant sects, the Protestants are relatively pacifists.

Protestants and Islamists differ in their attitudes to toleration. By and large, the Protestants are tolerant while the Islamists are less so; the USA, for example, permits freedom of religious expression and attempts to prevent the state promoting one religion as superior to any other. As against this, most of the Muslim countries are far less tolerant.

Differences in the two monolithic religions can be cited in abundance. But that apart, what is more significant here is that Islamic fundamentalism is more potent, and more severe than Christian fundamentalism.

❑ PAST 8 ATTEMPTS IGNOU QUESTIONS

Dec 2020: E-1: Discuss the meaning characteristics & kinds of Fundamentalism.

Answer by India Ebook: **Haywood** (Political Ideologies) defines fundamentalism as "a belief in the original or most basic principles of a creed, often associated with fierce commitment and sometimes reflected in fanatical zeal".

The **implications** of the **fundamentalism** are:

1) the belief either in the original creed or in its basic principles;

2) the belief takes the form of commitment and

3) the commitment takes the form of fanaticism.

Religion has been traditionally one of the major components of national identity, and at times, its most prominent feature. Almost every state comprises of groups having faith in one religion or the others: **Northern Ireland** has Protestants and Catholics.

Sri Lanka, Christian, Tamils and Buddhist Sinhalese, **India**, Hindus, Muslims, Sikhs, Christians and many others, and even in a particular religion, there may be one sect or the other: the Sunnis and the Shias among-the Muslims; the Arya Samajis, the Sanatan Dharmees and the Parnamis among the Hindus, for example.

In addition to **religious** fundamentalism, there is or what may be said, **secularist** fundamentalism, if fundamentalism is to be meant an uncompromising belief in the original and most basic thought frameworks of certain principles and a commitment to them. So understood, totalitarianism in the form of fascism or communism amounts to fundamentalism.

Religious fundamentalism and secularist fundamentalism have much in **common**: conviction in the basic principles, commitment to beliefs and more or less, a fanatical zeal in methods. Fundamentalism is not necessarily always religious, it may be non-religious as well. Fundamentalism is rigid conformity to doctrines and this may be religious or ideological or both.

Fundamentalism, though used so frequently in the present day world, has never been clear in the minds of the people so far as its meaning is concerned. The word means different things to different people. At times, it is used in a deprecatory sense without assigning any clear-cut connotation.

The word first received currency from a series of publications entitled, 'The Fundamentals' published in the linited States in 1909. Originally it indicated a belief that the Bible or for that matter any holy book of any religion is infallible as it contains the words of God. A fundamentalist regards his own creed or religion or a system of belief to be necessary, sufficient and eternally/completely valid.

One of the basic characteristics of fundamentalism is that it goes back to the original and to the definite sources and interprets them in its own words, asserting in the correctness of what the interpreter is saying.

A fundamentalist's position, in this regard, is that what he is saying is the correct interpretation of the original or that the source meant what his interpretation is; a fundamentalist would not accept the opposite interpretation nor would he like to change what he thinks to be correct.

Doctrinal conformity is another characteristic feature of all fundamentalism. The fundamentalist's conviction in the doctrine is unassailable, its principles are inviolable, indefeasible, literal and absolutely binding.

Fundamentalism does not know the language of conversation, but only that of imposition. Believing in doctrinal correctness, a fundamentalist wants the rest of the society to conform to the doctrine.

Fundamentalism is always without a base. It starts with a conclusion and, thereafter, searches for evidence of support for the conclusion and if the fundamentalist does not find any, he creates one. It is an evidence-less exercise.

Dec 2018: E-1: Write short note on: (d) Religious Fundamentalism.

Answer by India Ebook: Exact same as **Q.5** of Above.

23. MPS-001: UNIT-23: Nationalism

- Introduction
- What is Nationalism?
  - National Identity
- Theories of Nationalism
- **Perennial Theories:** Primordialist and Socio-Biological Theories
- **Modernization Theories:**
  - Social Communication theories (Deutsch, Rustow, Roklcan and Anderson)
  - Economistic Theories; Gellner's Theory of Nationalism;
  - Political Ideological Theories
- Rise arid Growth of Nationalism
  - Nation-state in Europe
  - Nation-state in America
  - Anti-Colonial Nationalism
- Contemporary Developments: Nationalism vis-a-vis Ethnic Resurgence and Globalization
- Book Exercise & Past 8 Attempts Questions

THEORIES OF NATIONALISM
[Q. 3, Q.4 and Q.5 of Book] Dec 2020

The most **hotly debated** question in the _context of nationalism_ is **when** and **how** did the **nation appear**.

In other words, **whether** national consciousness and sentiment is an evolutionary historical continuum **or** it is the result of modernism such as commercialization, industrialization, urbanization, mass participation in political culture etc.

Different theories of nationalism try to answer this question, though we **do not find** as **final answer**.

Primordlalist and Socio-Biological

Among the perennial theories, we can refer to the primordial and the socio-biological perspectives. Primordialism assumes that group identity is given; that there exist in all societies certain primordial, irrational attachments based on blood, race, language, religion, region etc.

Modern states particularly but not exclusively, in the third world, are superimposed on the primordial realities which are the ethnic groups or communities.

Primordialists believe that ethnic identity is deeply rooted in the historical experience of human beings to the point of being practically given. They believe that ethnic bonds are 'natural', fixed by the basic experiences that human beings undergo within their family ties and other primary groups.

In short, according to **Geertz**, i) primordial identities are given or natural, ii) primordial identities are ineffable, that is, cannot be explained or analysed by referring to social interaction but are coercive, iii) primordial identities deal essentially with the sentiments or affections.

The **social biologists** go a step further. This approach starts with the assumption that nationalism is the result of the extension of kin selection to a wider sphere of individuals who are defined it terms of putative or common descent. It insists that nationalism combines both rational and irrational elements; that is, a 'primitive mind' with modern techniques. The word nationalism expresses different realities: a love of country, the assertion of national identity and national dignity as well as the xenophobic obsession.

Social Communication Theories (Deutsch, Rustow, Rokkan and Anderson)

A pioneering study on the effects of modernization on nationalism was **Karl Deutsch's** nationalism, Social Communication. Here, he deals with the growth of nations & nationalism in the context of transition from traditional to modern societies. He emphasized the centrality of communication in the making of national communities. He focuses on the development of internal communications within the state as leading to the creation of a common sense of moral & political identity.

Another writer who has established a link between modernization and nationalism is the American political scientist **Dankwart Rustow**. In his book A World of Nations, he, writes that the essential link between modernization and nationalism consists of course in the need for an intensive division of labour. Other key features such as equality and loyalty have also been essential to the nation that emerged from the modernization process.

Another scholar **Stein Rokkan** has proposed a longue-duree which places some important variables in the medieval and early modern periods. In the modern situation, he accounts for the accelerated nation building in the 19th & 20th centuries by reference to six factors: i) combination of rural and urban resources, ii) spread and localization of industrialization, iii) pressure towards centralization and unification of the state, iv) pull of imperialist tendencies. v) tension between centre and periphery during the course of ethnic/linguistic mobilization, and vi) the conflict between the state and the church.

According to **Anderson**, national consciousness was made possible with the breakdown of three defining characteristics of pre-modern period: sacred scripts, divine kingship, and conflation of history with cosmology. He defines nation as an 'imagined political community'. His argument about the origin of nationalism leads to the focus on the tremendous impact of print capitalism.

Economistic Theories – Marxist & Non-Marxist

Economism is an extremely popular form of explanation and as such is favoured by both the **Marxists** & the **Non-Marxists**. In modern literature, this explanatory framework appears in different forms, but in final analysis the common denominator is that both deny the specificity of nation state.

Marxist theories envisage nationalism as a modern phenomenon and post a more or less explicit causal connection between the development of capitalism and the appearance of nationalism. For Karl Marx, nations and states need to be studied and evaluated within the context and from the perspective of their place in class relations and in the class struggle occurring on the global scale.

Another original Marxist approach to nationalism has been expounded by **Miroslav Hroch**. In his book **"Social Preconditions of National Revival of Europe"**, he has proposed a class analysis of modern nation as well as the role of cultural development.

He distinguished **three main states** in the development of modern society:

i) an early period in which the transition from feudalism to capitalism took place.

ii) the second stage coincided with the victory & consolidation of capitalism as well as the appearance of an organised working class movement and

iii) during the 20th century, there is a process of world wide integration & unprecedented development of mass communication.

At **cultural level**, each nationalist movement runs through **three phases:**

i) the period of scholarly interest,

ii) period of patriotic agitation and

iii) period of mass movement.

Political Ideological Theories

Apart from the economistic theories, there are a number of politico-ideological theories of nationalism. The common feature of all these theories is that they give a prominent role to the state in the development of nationalism in modernity. Under these theories, we shall dwell upon the views of four authors; namely, John Breuilly, Anthony Giddens, Paul Brass and Michael Mann.

John Breuilly in his book **Nationalism** and **State** accepts the existence of nations and nationalist sentiments in medieval Europe, but he restricts nationalism to the modern period and associates it with the development of modern state and of the international state system.

Nationalism is understood as a <u>form of politics</u> that arises in close association with the development of the state. In other words, in all its history, the modern state has shaped nationalist politics. Giddens defines nationalism as 'the existence of symbols and beliefs which are either propagated by elite groups or held by many of the members of regional, ethnic or linguistic categories of a population and which imply a community between them'.

Another writer **Paul Brass** insists that ethnicity and nationalism are the product of modernity and emphasizes its constructed character. According to him, cultures are fabricated by elite groups who use raw materials from different groups to create ethnics and nations.

To account for the development of **nationalism**, it is necessary to refer to all the four sources of social powers; namely, economic, political, ideological and military. In the first phase which began in the **16th century**, ideological power dominated. It was in the shape of religion and it gave form to proto-nations like Protestant England.

CONTEMPORARY DEVELOPMENTS: NATIONALISM VIS-A-VIS ETHNIC RESURGENCE & GLOBALIZATION

[Q.8 of Book] Dec 2019

Since the Second World War, three developments have affected the concept of nationalism which has been pointing to different directions.

The 1st was a consolidation trend which made the nation-state the main source of political authority. The domination of the nation-state, the most powerful form of political organisation, has been extended by the virtual end of colonial empires. There were 51 states in1945 whereas by1992, this number had gone up to 185.

The 2nd development relates to ethnic resurgence. Along with the consolidation of the nation state, there has been a revival of minority nationalist movements claiming measures of autonomy within the state or even independence from it.

Such conflicting trends have increased since the 1970s when the UK saw the growth of nationalist parties in Scotland & Wales, France experienced demands for measures of cultural autonomy from groups in Britain & Corsica.

The 3rd development relates to the process of globalization. During the last two decades, the world has become highly inter-dependent. Today, the nation-state has to operate in an inter-dependent world.

Information, money, weapons, technology, pollution, values, radiation, food, computers, drugs, disease, data - all flow rapidly around the globe giving the individual nation-states more opportunities, but also posing more threat to-their identity. Simultaneously, role of UNO, World Bank, IMF, GATT & NGOs is increasing by leaps & bounds.

Since the Second World War, three developments have affected the concept of nationalism which has been pointing to different directions.

The 1st was a consolidation trend which made the nation-state the main source of political authority. The domination of the nation-state, the most powerful form of political organisation, has been extended by the virtual end of colonial empires. There were 51 states in1945 whereas by1992, this number had gone up to 185.

The **2nd** development relates to ethnic resurgence. Along with the consolidation of the nation state, there has been a revival of minority nationalist movements claiming measures of autonomy within the state or even independence from it.

Such conflicting trends have increased since the 1970s when the UK saw the growth of nationalist parties in Scotland & Wales, France experienced demands for measures of cultural autonomy from groups in Britain & Corsica.

The **3rd** development relates to the process of globalization. During the last two decades, the world has become highly inter-dependent. Today, the nation-state has to operate in an inter-dependent world.

Information, money, weapons, technology, pollution, values, radiation, food, computers, drugs, disease, data - all flow rapidly around the globe giving the individual nation-states more opportunities, but also posing more threat to-their identity. Simultaneously, role of UNO, World Bank, IMF, GATT & NGOs is increasing by leaps & bounds.

Solved IGNOU Book Exercise & Solved Past 8 Attempts Questions

❑ **IGNOU BOOK EXERCISE**

4) Enumerate the **various theories** of nationalism. **(Dec-2020)**

Answer by India Ebook: The Answer is marked in the Summary Concept of this Unit.

8) Discuss **contemporary** developments in the arena of nationalism. **(Dec-2019)**

Answer by India Ebook: The Answer is marked in the Summary Concept of this Unit

❑ **PAST 8 ATTEMPTS IGNOU QUESTIONS** - 2 Questions asked in last 8 attempts as Marked above.

24. MPS-001: UNIT-24: Multi-Culturalism

Multiculturalism: The Concept
- ❑ The Ideal of Non-Discrimination
- ❑ Protecting Cultural Diversity
- ❑ Multiculturalism, Pluralism & Diversity

Multiculturalism & Liberalism – Critique of Liberal Democracies; Multiculturalism as a Liberal Theory of Minority Rights
The Idea of Differentiated Citizenship – Different Kinds of Special Rights; Differentiating Between Minorities
Critique of Multiculturalism
Multiculturalism-An Assessment

SKIP THIS UNIT FOR DEC 2022.

Solved IGNOU Book Exercise & Solved Past 8 Attempts Questions

❑ **IGNOU BOOK EXERCISE**

1) Explain the concept of multiculturalism in your own words. (June 2019, June 2021- 1ˢᵗ Part, June 2022)

Answer by India Ebook: Refer IGNOU Book.

2) Critically examine multiculturalism-liberalism interface.

Answer by India Ebook: Refer IGNOU Book.

4) Discuss the critiques of multiculturalism. (June 2021 – 2ⁿᵈ Part)

Answer by India Ebook: Refer IGNOU Book.

5) How will you assess multiculturalism?

Answer by India Ebook: Refer IGNOU Book.

❑ **PAST 8 ATTEMPTS IGNOU QUESTIONS - 2 Questions asked in last 8 attempts as Marked above.**

25. MPS-001: UNIT-25: Fascism

Introduction

Fascism - Meaning and an Ideational Profile

The Fascist Worldview

- ❑ **Core Ideas**
- ❑ **The Operational Dynamics**

Fascism and Challenges to Contemporary Life

Fascism - An Evaluation

Exercise & **Past 8 Attempts** Questions

THE FASCIST WORLD VIEW: Core Ideas [Q.1 of Book] Dec 2018

Irrationalism:

Irrationalism constitutes the fundamental layer of the fascist world-view. Fascism suggests to repudiate reason and objective science. The complexities of life are such a fascist would argue, that ordinary minds can not grapple with it. Peace and objectivity would not help in conquering the complexities surrounding the human life.

Fascism drew ideational sustenance from such varied sources as Plato, Rousseau, Hegel and George Sorel to erect the structures of irrationalism. For Mussolini, Hitler etc. stirring the people for action with no provable value or goal sanctity was enough. "Feel, don't think" was their consistent command to their followers.

Indiscriminate use of myths was also employed by the proponents of fascism. In particular, the myth of volk was most assiduously articulated by fascism.

Racialism:

Strange though it may be, Hitler based his social theory on the works of a French scholar Arthur de Gobineau, who was sent to Germany by France as a diplomat. His influence with the German led him to develop his theory of racial superiority which ultimately had a great impact on German history. Hitler categories the peoples of the world into three racial categories:

1) The culture creating race (e,g. Aryans)

2) The culture bearing race (e.g. Lastius, Slaves, the Orientals)

3) The culture destroying races (Gypsies, Negroes, Jews)

Statism - Drives towards a Corporate State:

The notion of Volkish spirit guided the course of state formation under fascism. The fascist statism drew heavily from totalitarianism, a term used by Mussolini himself. He raised the stature of the state as the "**Will of Wills**", the "**Good of Goods**" and the "**Soul of Souls**".

As such, the state can make any demand, give any order, require any sacrifice and the people must obey and comply with. State, argued **Mussolini**, happens to be the "**Creator of Rights**" and the "**Good of Goods**".

Hitler, even while according a somewhat secondary status to the state, maximised the totalitarian ethos under his regime. He successfully converted every possible medium as a political tool and decisively ensured that it catered to the priorities set forth by his regime.

The *fascist conception* of state authority had the foundation of a corporate state structure. This & other such trends will be taken up in the next section dealing with the operational dynamics of fascism.

Elitism:

Fascism drew legitimacy from the *notion of elitism as well*. Both **Hitler** and **Mussolini** argued that people are essentially uneven in their mental make-up, physical strength and spiritual endowments.

As such, they cannot contribute evenly to *civic and state affairs*. Since their contribution is uneven, they cannot expect equal rewards for their dissimilar contributions to the society and the state.

THE FASCIST WORLD VIEW: The Operational Dynamics
*Q4 of Book

In operational terms, *Fascism of Italy* & *Nazism of Germany* is regarded as 'totalitarianism of the right because fascism organised itself on behalf of many vested interests & against the left-wing parties & trade unions.

Centralization and Concentration of Power: The top government's organs centralized political power in both Italy and Germany. Accordingly, all sorts of provincial administrative mechanisms were systematically dismantled under the fascist regimes of Italy and Germany. Thus, fascism neither provided for federalism of any variety nor was there any type of separation of power.

Single Party: The **fascist party** in **Italy** and **NASDP** in Germany had highly centralized leaderships. These parties organized consent through intensive mobilization. The hierarchical levels of these parties were firmly controlled by the Duce and the Fuehrer respectively. Annual party congresses were festive gatherings for applauding the leader and confirming his policy guidelines.

Absolute Leadership: It was the envisaged role of the leader to amalgamate the people, the party and the state into one viable entity. The leader owed his authority through the built up charisma and personal traits.

Nazi Germany invented such slogans as "Leader is the party; the party is the leader" and "The leader ... knows the goals and the direction." The position of the leader was so invincible that Germany came to be known as the "Fuehrer-State", "the Leader-State". This was the highest mark of political absolutism.

Solved IGNOU Book Exercise & Solved Past 8 Attempts Questions

❏ IGNOU BOOK EXERCISE

1) Write an easy on 'the Fascist World-View'. [Dec 2018]

Answer by India Ebook: The Answer is marked in the Summary Concept of this Unit.

❏ PAST 8 ATTEMPTS IGNOU QUESTIONS - 2 Questions asked in last 8 attempts as 1 Marked above.

Another JUNE 2021: Write short note on Fascism

26. MPS-001: UNIT-26: Feminism

- ❖ Introduction; Types of Feminism
- ❖ **Patriarchy** - Views of Kate Millet; Gerda Lerner's Views; Control over Women's Sexuality and Labour Power; Different Forms
- ❖ **The Sex/Gender Distinction** - Sex is to Nature as Gender is to Culture; Masculinity, Femininity and Cultural Differences; Sexual Division of Labour and Work place; Ideological Assumptions behind Sexual Division of Labour
- ❖ **Developments in the Sex/Gender Distinction in Feminist Theory** - Views of Scholars like Alisan Jagger; Radical Feminists; Post-Modernist View; Gender Identity Interface; Naturalness of Heterosexually Questioned.
- ❖ Feminist Critique of the Public/Private Dichotomy - Feminist Criticism; Lack of Consensus Among Feminists

INTRODUCTION

The origins of the term feminism are not clear. There are several opinions, but the generally accepted version is that it was first used by the Utopian Socialist Charles Fourier in the 19th century, to refer to the question of equal rights for women.

In the West, women emerged in the early 19th century as a distinct interest group, partly because by that time it was clear that the promise of equality made by the bourgeois democratic revolutions of the 17th & 18th centuries excluded women, & partly because the Industrial Revolution had led to the increasingly visible presence of women in public employment.

In other parts of the world, the emergence of this question in the public arena was in the context of anti-imperialist movements and struggles against feudal oppression. Thus, feminist interventions in post-colonial societies had to engage with both the old oppression of tradition as well as the new oppression of colonialism.

TYPES OF FEMINISM: There are three (3) streams - liberal, socialist and radical feminism.

Liberal feminism is understood to work within the framework of the liberal state, theorising equality, freedom and justice in the context of liberal philosophy, pointing out that these concepts are inadequate until the gender dimension is taken into account.

Socialist Feminism links women's oppression to class society, and their critique draws from the Marxist categories of analysis, while simultaneously being critical of gender-blindness in Marxist theory.

Radical feminism theorises patriarchy as a system of male dominance independent of and prior to all other systems of domination - that is, in the radical feminist understanding, all other forms of exploitation and oppression are in a sense shaped by oppression based on sex, since that is historically the oldest form of oppression.

PATRIARCHY

This term is central to feminist analysis, and refers to an overarching system of male dominance.

Views of Kate Millet: Kate Millet, one of the earliest radical feminists to use the term in the 1970s, developed on sociologist Max Weber's conception of domination to argue that throughout history the relationship between the sexes has been one domination & subordination, in which men have exercised domination in two forms - through social authority & economic force. The emphasis is on patriarchy as a system, to establish that men's power over women is not an individual phenomenon, but is part of a structure.

Gerda Lerner's Views: The historian Gerda Lerner defines patriarchy thus: "the manifestations & institutionalisation of male dominance over women & children in the family and the extension of male dominance over women in society in general. It implies that men hold power in all the important institutions in society and that women are deprived of access to such power." This does not mean that every individual man is always in a dominant position and that every individual woman is always in a subordinate position.

Control over Women's Sexuality & Labour Power: Apart from control of women's sexuality under patriarchy through strictly policed institution of monogamous marriage, women's labour power is also controlled by men. Women's productivity within the household & outside is controlled by men who will determine whether women will work outside the household or not.

Different Forms: Patriarchy takes different Forms in different geographical regions and different historical periods. For instance, as the historian Uma Chakravarty has pointed out, the experience of patriarchy is not the same among tribal women a among women in highly stratified caste society. It is not the same today as it was in the 19th century, and it is not the same in India as it is in the industrialised countries of the West.

THE SEX/GENDER DISTINCTION

Sex is to Nature as Gender is to Culture: One of the key contributions of feminist theory is the making of a distinction between "sex" and "gender". Sex as referring to the biological differences between men and women and gender as indicating the vast range of cultural meanings attached to that basic difference.

Masculinity, Femininity and Cultural Differences: Feminist anthropologists, pre-eminent among whom is Margaret Mead, have demonstrated that what is understood as masculinity and femininity varies across cultures. In other words, not only do different societies identify a certain set of characteristics as Feminine and another set as masculine. But also, these characteristics are not the same across different cultures. Thus, feminists have argued that there is no necessary co-relation between the biology of and women and the qualities that are thought to be Masculine & Feminine.

Sexual Division of Labour and Work Place: This sexual division of labour is not limited to the home, it exteneds even to the "public" arena of paid work, and again, this has nothing to do with "sex" (biology) and everything to do with "gender" (culture). Certain kinds of work considered to be "women's work", and other kinds men's, but more important is the fact that whatever work that women do, gets lower wages and is less valued.

Ideological Assumptions behind Sexual Division of Labour:

The fact is that it is not a "natural" biological difference that has behind the sexual division of labour, but curtain ideological assumptions. So on the one land, women are supposed to be physically weak and unlit for heavy manual labour. But both in the home and outside, they do the heaviest of work- carrying heavy loads of water and firewood, grinding corn, transplanting paddy, carrying head-loads in mining and construction work.

DEVELOPMENTS THE SEX/GENDER DISTINCTION IN FEMINIST THEORY

Broadly, we can discern four main ways in which the sex/gender distinction has been further developed in feminist theory.

Views of Scholars like Alisan Jagger

Scholars like Alison Jagger argue that "sex" and "gender" are dialectically and inseparably related, and that the, conceptual distinction that the earlier feminists established between the two is not sustainable beyond a point.

In this understanding, human biology is constituted by a complex interaction between the human body, the physical environment and the state of development of technology and society. Thus, Jaggar puts it, "the hand is as much the product of labour as the tool of labour."

This is trite in two senses. One, in a long-term evolutionary sense, over the millennia. That is, human bodies have evolved differently in different parts of the globe, due to differences in diet, climate and the nature of work performed.

Two, in a more short-term sense, in one lifetime that is, it is now recognised that neurophysiology and hormonal balances are affected by social factors like anxiety, physical labour, and the level and kind of social interaction, just as much as social interaction is affected by people's neurophysiology and hormonal balances.

When we apply this understanding, that biology and culture are interrelated, to the sex/gender distinction, the, relevant implication is that women's bodies have been shaped by social restrictions and by norms of beauty. That is, the "body" has been formed as much by "culture" as by "nature".

In short, we must consider that there are two equally powerful factors at work - one, there is a range of interrelated ways in which society produces sex differences and two, sex differences structure society in particular ways.

Radical Feminists

A second kind of rethinking of sex/gender has come from radical feminism which argues that feminists must not underplay the biological difference between the sexes and attribute all difference to "culture" alone.

To do so is to accept the male civilization's devaluing of the female reproductive role. This is a criticism of the liberal feminist understanding that in an ideal world, men and women would be more or less alike.

Radical feminists claim that on the contrary, patriarchal social values have denigrated "feminine" qualities and that it is the task of feminism to recover these qualities, and this difference between men and women, as valuable.

The radical feminist position on the sex/gender distinction is that there are certain differences between men and women that arise from their different biological reproductive roles, and that therefore, women are more sensitive, instinctive and closer to nature.

Radical feminists such as Susan Griffin and Andrea Dworkin, for example, believe that women's reproductive biology, the process of gestation and the experience of mothering, fundamentally affects their relationship to the external world.

In this context, it is interesting to note that some scholars are of the opinion that the strictly bipolar model of masculinity/femininity and the devaluing of the feminine are characteristic of only the modern western civilization.

Post-Modernist View: A more recent feminist position takes the opposite view from that of radical feminists. While radical feminists argue that the sex/gender distinction underplays sex differences, a school of postmodern feminisit thought holds that, it over-emphasizes the biological body.

Gender Identity Interface: A 4th kind of rethinking of the sex/gender distinction comes from locating "gender" in a grid of identities-caste, class, race, religion. This would mean that the biological category of "women" does not necessarily have shared interests, life-situations, or goals.

This kind of understanding has arisen from political practice of women's movement all over world, which has increasingly shown up, fact that "women" don"t exist as a pre-existing subject which can simply be mobilized by women's movement.

In India, an example of this, is the debate over Uniform Civil Code. All religious communities have their own personal laws which discriminate against women on matters of marriage, divorce, inheritance and guardianship of children.

Naturalness of Heterosexuality Questioned: A further significant implication of the sex/gender distinction suggested by feminist theory is that the supposed naturalness of heterosexuality is called into question. Adrienne Rich uses the term "compulsory heterosexuality" to refer to the way in which heterosexual marriage is set up as the unquestionable norm.

If "male" and "female" as natural categories are challenged by feminist theory, then it offers simultaneously, a challenge to the whole range of institutionalised practices (marriage and family) through which patriarchal property and power relations are maintained. Thus, sexual identity and sexual orientation are important issues for contemporary feminist theory.

FEMINIST CRITIQUE OF THE PUBLIC/PRIVATE DICHOTOMY

In liberal theory the distinction between "public" and "private" answers the question of the legitimate extent of the authority of the law. The public realm is understood in this context to be open to government regulation while the private realm is to be protected from such action - sexuality and the family being understood to be private.

In Marxist theory too, this distinction is central, although from a different point or view. Engels argued that women's oppression begins with the transformation of housework from a public to a private service.

Feminist Criticism

Feminist scholarship emerging from both liberal and Marxist traditions have contested this distinction as being conceptually flawed and politically oppressive. From within the liberal tradition comes the argument that the dichotomy assumed between "public" (non-domestic) and "private" (domestic) has enabled the family to be excluded from the values of "justice" and "equality" which have animated liberal thought since the 17th century-beginnings of liberalism.

The "individual" was the adult male head of the household, and thus his right to be free from interference by the state or church included his rights over those in his control in the private realm - women, children, servants. Thus, oppression within the family was rendered invisible to political theory.

In addition to sharing this view, socialist-feminists critique the public/private distinction in Marxist theory produced by the model of political economy based on "production", defined as economic production for the capitalist market.

This model, they argue, ignores the "private" sphere of "reproduction", where women are responsible for reproducing both humans (through child-bearing) and labour power (through housework). For traditional Marxists, this work is seen to be part of the non-economic or super structural realm, and is not even defined as "work". Socialist feminists therefore, contest the public/private distinction by showing that sexuality, procreation, and housework, understood to be "private", in fact hold up the "public" sphere of production.

Their arguments that housework is a commodity - it is unpaid labour that helps to reproduce labour power. This is so in two senses:

a) when male labour comes home, it is the housework done by women that ensures that they can go back to work the next day

b) the bearing of children reproduces actual people who will work in factories etc.

However, this work is not paid for, and this unpaid labour in the "private" sphere underlies and ensures capitalist production in the "public" sphere.

Thus, feminists across the political spectrum are agreed that the public and the private are not two distinct and separate spheres and that the assumption that they are, is uniformly detrimental to women's interests.

IGNOU Book Exercise & Past 8 Attempts Questions - IMPORTANT

❑ IGNOU BOOK EXERCISE

FOR THIS CHAPTER READ THE FULL CONCEPT ABOVE
1) Trace the origin of the term feminism.

2) Enumerate the different types of feminism. What is common to different feminist positions? (Dec 2018)

❑ **PAST 8 ATTEMPTS IGNOU QUESTIONS - 1 Questions asked in last 8 attempts as Marked above.**

27. MPS-001: UNIT-27: Gandhism and Pacifism

Introduction; Gandhism; Pacifism; The Relevance of Pacifism

Solved IGNOU Book Exercise & Solved Past 8 Attempts Questions

Dec 2020: Discuss Gandhi's views on non-violence.

Answer by India Ebook: Mahatma Gandhi is a religious humanist. For the attainment of *Swaraj*, he has worked out certain principles that are woven into political philosophy by others. These principles of Gandhi are known as **Gandhism**.

Gandhi had neither the time nor the patience to formulate any 'theory' with the result what we have today is a collection of speeches, articles and other writings, which are not 'theory', but, at best, the background for a sound theory.

Gandhi has an alternative to the Liberal as well as Marxist ideology. The development of the ideas of Gandhi after him and their application become important as a solution oriented mechanism to save humanity.

Gandhi says that non-violence is **not merely a personal virtue**. It is also a social virtue to be cultivated like the other virtues. Surely, society is largely regulated by the expression of non-violence in its mutual dealings.

What I ask for is *an extension* of it on a larger, national and international scale. All society is held together by non-violence, even as the earth is held in her position by gravitation. But when the law of gravitation was discovered, the discovery yielded results of which our ancestors had no knowledge.

Even so, when *society* is deliberately constructed in accordance with the law of non-violence, its structure will be different in material particulars from what it is today. But I cannot say in advance what the government based on non-violence will be like.

What is **happening today** is disregard of the Law of non-violence and enthronement of violence as if it were an eternal law. A society based on non-violence can only consist of groups settled in villages in which voluntary co-operation is the condition of dignified and peaceful existence.

Although *Gandhi is not* the originator of non-violent struggle, he is a major historical player in its refinement and development. Gandhi also recognizes importance of strategy-skillfullness in the choice and use of means and methods to increase the possibilities of success in non-violent struggle.

He has contributed significantly to the refinement of strategy and the practice of careful strategic planning for this type of conflict. He has brought greatly increased strategic sophistication to the technique.

As per Gandhi's lessons for us to overcome multiple conflicts, the following ideas are important:

a) Justice and freedom require empowering oppressed people and redistributing power in society.

b) Peace is not achieved by stifling conflicts in which important issues are at stake, but by using non-violet struggle to fight those conflicts to the point of resolution.

c) Mass non-violent struggle in politics is possible as a substitute for both passivity and violence.

d) Masses of people who will never accept non-violence as a moral principle will at times practice pragmatic non-violent struggle.

e) The key to widespread adoption of non-violent means has in formulating and implementing strategies of non-violent struggle to serve as substitute for violence for specific purposes.

f) Non-violent struggles can be made significantly more effective if wise strategies with implementing tactics are developed and applied.

g) Non-violent struggles can be developed, refined, adapted in a series of specific replacements to be a substitute for violence as a final means of applying pressure and power in society and politics.

28. MPS-001: UNIT-28: Communitarianism & Civic Republicanism

- Introduction
- Communitarianism: An Introduction
- The Value of Community Membership
- The Communitarian Position on State Neutrality
- Civic Republicanism: An Introduction
- The Idea of Republican Freedom
- The Idea of Republican Government

COMMUNITARINISM: INTRODUCTION

The communitarian perspective developed and became central to political theory during the 1980s with the publication of Michael Sandel's Liberalism and the Limits of Justice (1982). In this book, Sandel develops one of the most forceful critiques of Rawlsian liberalism, the statement of which is found in John Rawls's A Theory of Justice (1971). Other political thinkers who have contributed to the development of communitarianism, although in different ways are Alisdair MacIntyre, Michael Walzer, Charles Taylor and Will Kymlicka.

Communitarians are first and foremost concerned with community. Two or more people may be understood to constitute a community when they share a common conception of the good and see, this good as partly constitutive of their identity or selves. Such a "constitutive community" may be a close friendship, family relationship, neighbourhood or even a comprehensive political community.

Since people are free, rational and capable of self-determination, their interests are better promoted by letting them choose for themselves what sort of life they want to lead.

In the communitarian view, it is not enough to think in terms of a two-level relationship with the individual at one level and the state at the other. Groups and communities occupy an important intermediate position between the individual and the state and should be included among the kinds of rights and duty bearing units whose interrelationships are explored.

THE VALUE OF COMMUNITY MEMBERSHIP

A great deal of communitarian thought has presented itself in terms of an espousal of the value and importance of community membership to both peoples' lives in general, and to the decisions they make in the political sphere in particular. Such an espousal is made with an explicit reference to and a whole rejection of the individualistic conception of the self.

The essence of the communitarian claim is that in defining its as individuals, liberal individualism places us at a distance, in fact detaches us from our social ends and conceptions of the good in a way that simply fails to correspond to the way in which we actually relate to these ends.

Such a conception of the self, as detached and separate from social ends, is according to communitarians, disputable on two grounds: first, that it devalues, discounts and downgrades the importance of community membership; and second, that it presents a flawed understanding of the relation between the self and its ends.

On the first criticism, communitarianism challenges liberal individualism for downgrading and discounting the importance of community. More specifically, they criticize individualism for ignoring the extent to which it is the society or community which people live in that shape who they are and the values they have.

On the second criticism, communitarianism attacks individualism for holding a mistaken or false understanding of the relationship between the self and its ends - one that sees individual ends and conceptions of the good to be formed independently and prior to society.

CIVIC REPUBLICANISM : AN INTRODUCTION

Civic republican political theory takes its starting point from a long established tradition of thinking about politics-a tradition that is understood to have contributed significantly to the development of democracy.

The term republicanism is defined and understood in contrast with monarchy or the personal rule of kings and emperors. Whereas a monarch enjoys personal authority over his subjects and rules his realm as his personal possession and more or less to realize his personal interests, government in a republic is, in principle, the common business of the citizens conducted by them for realizing the common good. The idea of republicanism, thus, develops from a desire and the attempt to replace 'the empire of men with the empire of law'.

The civic republican perspective begins by adopting some of the important ideas of Greek political thought. In fact, civic republicanism begins, as does Greek political thinking, from the premise that man is by nature a social-political animal. Men, however, are also moral beings as they embody certain moral purposes. Naturally therefore, and in order to realize their interests and develop their true selves, men must live together in a political association, more specifically in a self-governing political community.

A self-governing political community is one in which citizens participate to realize the good of both the individual as well as the collective. In a republic then, citizens are essentially virtuous as they place the common good above their particular individual goods. Underlying and contributing to the civic republican ideal of a good polity are somewhat distinct ideas of freedom and government - ideas, which republicans conclude, go beyond and are deeper than the dominant liberal notions of freedom and government.

THE IDEA OF REPUBLICAN FREEDOM

At the heart of civic republicanism is a distinct and supposedly rich idea of freedom. According to republican theorists, this idea of freedom contributes to the discourse on freedom by going beyond the traditional dominant liberal conception of freedom. To understand the distinctness and contributions of this idea, it would be helpful to give a summarized account of the traditional conceptions of freedom.

According to the civic republican tradition, the distinction between negative and positive freedom, between the liberty of the ancients and the liberty of the moderns, fails to capture the true essence and value of freedom. As an alternative, republican theorists develop and advocate the idea of republican freedom. Republican freedom, they argue, although a kin to the traditional distinction, transcends it to deliver a richer and more valid account of freedom.

Underlying the republican notion of freedom as non-domination is an understanding of the meaning of domination as well as its relationship with interference. Domination, as understood by the republicans, is the ability and capacity of one agent to exercise power over the other, particularly the power of arbitrary interference.

The relationship between domination and interference, according to republicans. is deeper as well as more problematic than is apparent. Domination, as they argue, can be experienced and exercised without actual interference, such as experienced by the lucky slave.

THE IDEA OF REPUBLICAN GOVERNMENT

Based on the republican idea of freedom as non-domination is the idea of republican government. Freedom as non-domination, as republicans believe, would be achieved only when each citizen feels that he/she is not being ruled or dominated by the power of others, but by his/her own interests.

As such, republican freedom is the desire not to rule but rather not to be ruled. This, republicans believe, necessitates a different & a more inclusive idea of government. Below, we examine the idea of a republican government.

Underlying the idea of the republican government are the principle of civic virtue, the idea of common & the notion of active civic participation. The republican idea of civic virtue may be understood as he willingness to set the common good above one's own or family's interests.

In fact, the idea of citizens being virtuous is an integral part of the tradition of civic republicanism. Civic republicanism, in a similar vein with communitarians, requires that we as citizens place the common good above our particular individual interests.

While the republican doctrine lays great stress on the fundamental importance of civic virtue, it lays equal stress on the fragility of virtue- the danger that a people or its leaders would become corrupt, thereby threatening the republic. The republican idea of citizenship, however, ought to be contrasted with the liberal idea of citizenship. The advocacy of the ideas of civic virtue, common good, active civic citizenship, mixed constitutions and separation of powers make up an important, if not the core of the idea of republican government.

Solved IGNOU Book Exercise & Solved Past 8 Attempts Questions

❑ IGNOU BOOK EXERCISE

Read the Concept only.

29. MPS-001: UNIT-29: Political Theory in a Globalising World

- Introduction
- How does Political Theory Evolve?
- Binaries in Political Theory: Liberalism and Marxism
- Modernism and Post-Modernism
- Epistemological Shift
- Globalization and Identity Politics (Refer MPS-003, Unit-17: Identity Politics in India)
- Synthesis in Political Theory
- Welfare State vs. Minimal State (Refer MPS-003, Unit-16: Welfare State)
- The Blurring of State Sovereignty
- Role of WTO, Multi-nationals and the NGOs (Refer MPS-002: IR)
- State vs. Civil Society (Refer MPS-001, Unit-10: State and Civil Society)
- Ethnic Cleavages
- New Dimensions in the Theory of Federalism

INTRODUCTION

The disintegration of socialist states in European Europe culminating in the **break-up of the mighty Soviet Union** marks the **triumph** of **liberalism over socialism**, democracy over one-party rule and laissez faire economies over centralized economy.

The bipolar world has given way to a **unipolar world**. In the wake of these developments, the world is witnessing fundamental changes in the form of liberalization, privatization and globalization. The trade barriers among the states are getting blurred and a globalized market is emerging. In centralized and mixed economies, the process of disinvestment and structural adjustments is leading to the shrinking of the public sector. How will these epochal changes manifest themselves in the form of newer concerns in Political Theory is an important question that needs to be considered.

HOW DOES POLTICAL THEORY EVOLVE?

At the very outset, we must understand as to how political theory emerges in any historical phase. **Every political theorist** begins to feel agitated about certain maladies in the society in which he lives & wants to find out remedies for these maladies. Thus, **Plato's** Ideal State is his response to the rotten state of Athens in which he lived.

Thomas Hobbes was worried at the violent and law-less conditions prevailing in 16th century England. Similarly, **Karl Marx** was full of anguish at the miserable conditions of the working class in the 19th Century Europe. Therefore, he urged this class to rise in Revolt & overthrow the Capitalist system.

BINARIES IN P0LTICAL THEORY: LIBERALISM & MARXISM

Before we spell out the nature of political theory in the era of globalization, it is necessary for us to understand the binary nature of modern and contemporary political theory out of which it will emerge. There are mainly **two grand ideological designs** in modern political theory: **Liberalism and Marxism**.

The liberal political theory emphasizes democratic governance where the people can articulate their problems and choices. It stands for universal human rights. It is wedded to the promotion of common good and it holds two human values - Liberty and Equality - as primary; although liberty often gets priority over equality.

Marxism, on the other hand, highlights the fact that all human societies are class-based societies consisting of the exploiters and the exploited. These two classes are constantly at war with each other and this war will consummate in a revolution leading to the final victory of the exploited class which will pave the way for the emergence of a class-less and stateless society.

In short, modern political theory is concerned with **universal goals** like Justice, Liberty and Equality. It attempts to identify the institutional structures of domination & tries to evolve strategies to demolish them.

It is, however, evident that these goals of Liberal & Marxist theory were never realized, at least not fully. In **liberal democracies**, participation of people remained only marginal & ruling power got concentrated in hands of political elite. The **socialist societies**, on the other hand, witnessed excessive centralization of power in the hands of the communist party leadership. The exploitation of the workers not only continued, but in some cases it became more intense.

MODERNISM & POST-MODERNISM

In recent years, an alternative to both these strands of modern political theory has appeared in the form of Post-Modernism. The post-modernists challenge liberalism for its abstract categories - like the universal rights of all people and emphasize the rights of specific groups women, tribal, blacks and the colonial people etc.

This has led to the emergence of **New Social Movements** which challenge specific forms of social domination based on gender, caste, colour and race. Identity politics has become the most crucial element in these movements. It also marks a shift from macro abstract political, social and economic issues to culture.

The basic argument identity politics is that individuals define themselves mainly as belonging to a given cultural group which perceives itself as disadvantaged and oppressed at the hands of groups which are privileged and dominant- males, upper castes, white races and the imperialist countries.

The relevant binary categories in identity policies become "we" and "they". It is important to note that in practical terms, this new political theory of identity politics tantamount to rejecting the Marxian category of "class" as a major tool of analysis.

It, equally vehemently, negates liberalism's universal categories like "universal rights", "civil liberties" and "equality". Instead of the mega "class war" of Marxian variety, it emphasizes "local struggles". Instead of advocating power to the working class it advocates empowerment of the local communities and specific cultural groups.

EPISTEMOLOGICAL SHIFT

In epistemological terms, this new political theory of the "post-modernist" variety **negates three basic methodological tenets** of modern political theory: holism/universalism, essentialism and reductionism. It is difficult to explain the full import of these terms. Briefly, we may say that the parts that constitute the whole. Thus, it talks in terms of macro instead of micro phenomena.

Essentialism underscores the importance of comprehending the general essence of the phenomenon rather the mere appearance of it. Reductionism in modern political theory refers to the tendency of reducing all analyses and explanations of a phenomenon to a single element or a single factor.

For example, in classical Marxism all economic divisions and all social and political hierarchies are reduced to "class" and the "economic factor" is considered as the only factor that determines the course of history. Thereby, the role of "ideas" and 'cultural identities" gets totally ignored or considerably under-played in modern political theory. The post-modernist political thinking, on the other hand, not only highlights "particularism", but also emphasises the relevance of several factors in comprehending a phenomenon.

Instead of "elite" history, it stands for "mass" history and subaltern studies. Instead of history from above, it is wedded to the idea of history from below. Post-modernism also has its own specific emancipatory agenda. Rejecting modern political theory's thrust for a systematic change, post-modernism stands for the emancipation of specific groups.

Solved IGNOU Book Exercise & Solved Past 8 Attempts Questions

1) What is Identity Politics?

Answer by India Ebook: Refer MPS-003: India: Democracy & Development, UNIT-17.